WEEP NOT FOR ME

(JESUS AND CHRISTIANITY)

by

F. R. BARRY

THE RELIGIOUS EDUCATION PRESS, LTD

(*A member of the Pergamon Group*)

HEADINGTON HILL HALL   OXFORD

PUBLISHER'S NOTE

It is the habit of our times to bemoan the fate of so many of the values and standards associated with the Christian religion; and indeed to bemoan the fate of Christianity itself. The former Bishop of Southwell here sets forth the implications of the Christian Gospel in such a way as to dispel the gloom of the pessimists. In the Risen Christ and his Gospel lies the hope of mankind. It is not Christ and his Gospel that is in jeopardy, but the world which rejects him. It is not he who is to be pitied, but we. He is not the victim but the victor.

Daughters of Jerusalem, weep not for me
But weep for yourselves and for your children.

© 1968 F. R. Barry

First published 1968

Made and printed in Great Britain by
Cox & Wyman, Ltd., London, Fakenham and Reading

08 006252 0. Paperback edition
08 006287 3. Hard cover edition

CONTENTS

PREFACE

THIS little book contains the substance of a course of popular lectures on the Gospels delivered in St. Michael's Church, Cornhill, under the St. Antholin Trust in the spring and autumn of 1966. In this form it is meant for someone in particular, whose importance I came to realize more and more in a long ministry, both as a priest and bishop – the man in the pew half-way down the church.

He is a believing and practising Christian, but he sits somewhere near the back of the church, rather than confidently up in front, because he is uncertain of his position. He is the perplexed twentieth-century layman. Exposed to a torrent of disturbing books about Difficulties and Objections, talk about Religionless Christianity and alarming phrases about the Death of God, and constantly bombarded by suggestions that Christianity is no longer credible, he wonders whether his faith can still be valid. And he has a suspicion, from what he has learnt by hearsay, that the critical work of scholars on the Gospels has undermined the historical foundations, and that the clergy are keeping something back from him.

What follows is an attempt to tell him something about the present state of New Testament criticism and the attitude to the Gospels which emerges from it, offering him grounds for a reasoned faith. At the same time, it is hoped that he may be liberated from a merely conventional and unthinking 'orthodoxy', under which our Lord has too often been disguised, and enabled to see him as a real Person.

It is neither honest nor possible today to write on these matters as though nothing had happened. A great deal has happened. We live in the nineteen sixties, and we must accept the demands of our own time and the new knowledge which God is giving to man both in the secular and the religious field. I am trying to give the man in the pew confidence, to show him that, despite all the difficulties – which I have certainly no desire to minimize – he may be frankly twentieth-century man and still continue to be a believing Christian.

Though it is intentionally elementary, there is more in this book than perhaps meets the eye. No one who knows anything of the subject can commit himself to *any* responsible statement about the content and meaning of the Gospels without having done some fairly laborious homework. There is probably not a sentence in what I have written which cannot be found, better said, in some other book. It makes no claim at all to originality, it depends throughout on specialist work by experts. And if anyone dares to write about Jesus Christ, it involves his whole theological position, and indeed his total philosophy of life. In a sense, the whole of his life must be behind it. Fifty years ago, I knew much more about New Testament scholarship than I do now – of course I have done my best to 'get it up' again – but I could not then have written these pages. May the reader for whom they are intended find something in them which may be of some help.

F. R. B.

Westminster,
February 1967.

1

CHRISTIANITY AND THE SECULAR

'SECULAR' is a blessed word today and it is heard, paradoxically enough, most frequently in religious circles. Nearly everywhere, Christianity is moving out from the sacristy to the market-place, from narrowly 'churchy' preoccupations to the life and work of the everyday world around it – industry, education, social welfare and all that makes up the framework of human existence – as we commonly say, of 'ordinary' life.

That is the world in which the Bible lives and in which Jesus Christ himself lived. Let us remind ourselves from the start that the Author of man's salvation was a layman, not any kind of ecclesiastical personage. When phrases are used like 'secular sanctity', Christianity 'in a secular context', what the word stands for is the rediscovery of something the Church ought never to have forgotten, for it is entailed in its doctrine of Creation – the fundamental truth that the world is God's world, that he is at work in it and has a purpose for it. This purpose is made known through Christ and his Church (Ephesians 3. 9–11) – which is here to serve and to sanctify it. In itself the word does not, or need not, imply any 'secularization' of Christianity.

Secular does not mean anti-religious. 'Secular' clergy, living 'in the world', as distinguished from 'regulars' under cloistral 'rule', were hardly supposed to be anti-Christian, even though it is true that the latter came to be technically called 'religious', that is, members of a religious order. It means non-sacral, non-ecclesiastical. (A school or hospital is a secular building, while a place of worship would be called religious, but the former may serve an essentially Christian end.) Church and State have frequently been in conflict, but in classical Christian theory the secular arm was an organ of the Christian society. The temporal power, no less than the spiritual, was ordained by God and answerable to God, as an instrument of social justice – a secular means to the fulfilment of God's purpose for the children of men.

However avowedly 'secular' life may be – secular in the sense of not acknowledging any ecclesiastical control – it is still, nevertheless, under God's law – that is surely implied in believing in God at all.

The world belongs to God and all that is in it; in his sovereignty there are no reserved territories. We are now, however, learning to understand that God has endowed the whole created order, and most evidently the human will, with a measure of relative freedom and independence. At the same time it is coming to be recognized that the various departments of human activity – art, science, politics and so forth – have their own relative autonomy, working by their own laws and methods within their own limiting conditions, which religion must respectfully accept as part of God's providential order.

But because they are not technically religious, that does not mean that they are exempt from reference to the ultimate moral and spiritual realities, or that they are not to be increasingly incorporated into the Kingdom of God. Nor does it mean that religion is 'irrelevant'. It means that religion cannot be departmentalized. It is not one particular kind of activity. Because we have allowed it to become that, people today think of it as marginal to the daily concerns and decisions of life in the world. It is a total orientation of the whole man. There are not two different kinds of activity, holy or sacred and secular or profane; there are two different attitudes to life, two different ways of response to our environment, one of which is religious and the other 'secular'.

From the eighteenth century onwards the West has been increasingly coming under the spell of a secularist philosophy of life. At first confined to private opinions of the privileged intellectual *élite*, it has now become the acknowledged world-view of the great majority of the population. The dictionary definition is 'the modern tendency to ignore, if not to deny, the principles of supernatural religion in the interpretation of the world and of existence'.[1] For all practical purposes there is no room for God in it. Indeed it is popularly assumed that science has made the traditional Christian belief at once unnecessary and incredible. Man can now control the world for himself without praying to God to do things for him, and the God-hypothesis is no longer needed. Every day we learn more about the laws of nature and we have discovered already that the universe works by its own internal causation, and is not manipulated *ab extra*.[2]

Men, having eaten of the tree of knowledge, have become, a the serpent promised, 'like gods'. Man, indeed, has taken the place of God and claims to direct his destiny for himself. Unlimited 'progress' in a man-made world, with scientific mythology for a religion – that is the faith of the twentieth century West. And, with the global extension of its techniques, the 'West' will soon mean nearly the whole world.

There was a time when it all seemed highly emancipated. Free from the fetters of ancient superstitions, Man could now enter into his kingdom and fashion a world safe for men to live in. But few thinking people would say that now. It has not brought the expected liberation. For the spirit of man cannot

[1] *Oxford Dictionary of the Christian Church* (O.U.P., 1957), which states that the term was first used by Holyoake (1817–1906) and was developed into extreme atheism in a more logical form by Bradlaugh.

[2] Science is concerned with secondary causes, of which, of course, the Bible knows nothing, not with final causes, meanings or values. The latter must be ruled out in advance. Scientists would be false to their vocation and their function in God's purpose for the world if they brought theology into their experiments. Their concern is with physical causation. Science, therefore, *qua* science, *must* be 'atheistic', and no experiment can answer questions which have been deliberately excluded from it.

On the other hand, the scientist himself may be, and often is, a convinced Christian who finds the ultimate explanation of everything, its meaning and value, in the will of God, who knows, therefore, that science has a moral end, and so conducts his 'godless' researches as part of his religion, to the glory of God. The popular mind has not properly grasped the distinction.

be contained within the physical process of nature. Though he lives in the natural process, man transcends it. Indeed, he could not be aware of the natural process, much less conduct scientific inquiries into it, if he were no more than a part of the natural process, any more than he could be aware of time if he were no more than a knot in the space-time process.

What it is to be man is to be person, spirit – a statement with which many Humanists would agree. We know a great deal more about spirit than we know about 'matter', whatever matter may be, for we all know ourselves, and we are spirits. Nature is impersonal, man is person. Nature is determined, man is free. Alone among nature's children he can make choices and pursue ideal, imagined satisfactions, identifying himself with his chosen ends. Thus he is always reaching out beyond himself towards that in his total environment which transcends him, which is yet insistently laying claim upon him and is partially disclosed in his experience, in truth, in beauty, in love, in moral judgements, and with which he seeks communion in worship. Only in what is beyond himself can he find true fulfilment.

But, having ruled out any transcendental reference, and self-imprisoned in a closed system of natural and social determinants, his spirit enclosed in a sub-personal process, modern man feels frustrated and 'estranged', from himself, his culture, his fellows and his existence, unable to find any real meaning in life, on an exclusively natural plane, at all. Futility, meaninglessness, absurdity – this is the burden of fiction and drama today. Man as spirit now thinks that he is alone in a mindless, impersonal and amoral process, with no status or foot-hold in the scheme of things – which seems to deny what he knows himself to be.

Existentialists make a gesture of defiance in a self-authentication of existence; and if they are atheists that is heroic courage. But there is no response from beyond themselves. ('There was no voice nor any that answered.') The deep feeling of spiritual insecurity, underlying the lack of conviction or any sense of imperative obligation which is so characteristic of our culture, reveals itself in a chronic anxiety-state – the endemic disease of contemporary society. Indeed it may not be fantastic to predict that modern civilization, like the ancient, may collapse through a radical 'loss of nerve'.

Man cannot believe in himself if he does not believe in something beyond himself. But when Jesus said to his followers 'Be not anxious', did he not intend more than not to worry about food and clothes and material necessities? Perhaps he meant 'Do not be afraid to live' – he was often saying 'Be of good cheer; be brave' – because you can trust the Reality at the heart of life.

How can men today find access to a faith which does not belittle the secular, yet transcends it? That, of course, is what Christianity claims to offer. Christianity is essentially supernatural – in traditional language, it 'comes down from heaven'; and if it ever ceases to be that, if it ever comes to be perfectly content with a purely secular and this-world outlook, then it will have nothing important left to say. It is not primarily a code of ethics. The ethic of Christianity is derivative from its faith in God and eternal life through Christ. Yet it is not an otherworldly mysticism. What might be called its constitutive dogma is the Word made flesh, the involvement of God in history – the Beyond disclosed to and within the secular, the Supernatural through and within the natural.

One of the biggest problems before the Churches is how to present a supernatural faith to a naturalistically-minded age. When Christians try to interpret their beliefs to non-believers, they very often fail. For religion, like science, has its own language; and, transferred into a different frame of reference, into a non-religious world-view, religious language may seem to be nonsensical – as philosophers have not been slow to point out.

To the modern man with his mind conditioned by science, the word supernatural acts like a red rag. What it suggests to him is the 'miraculous' in the wrong sense of portentous or irrational – some intervention, as it were, *ab extra* by a Deity 'up there' or 'out there', interrupting the ordered course of nature (as God has now taught men's minds to understand it) and thus denying some of man's greatest achievements and thrusting him back to pre-scientific darkness. Unfortunately, Christian thought and devotion has been fixated in imagery and symbols derived from pre-Christian literary conventions in the so-called 'apocalyptic' writings; and these are too often taken as descriptive – statements of fact or literal predictions.

But that is not what Christian teaching is talking about. The Man who said 'Consider the lilies ... how they grow' (Matthew **6.** 28), who refused to jump off the pinnacle of the Temple ['Thou shalt not tempt the Lord thy God' (Luke **4.** 12)] was not thinking in such terms as those. Nor has Christian theology, in its main stream, sanctioned them. But because of these associated overtones, Christians need to be scrupulous and vigilant in their thinking and speaking about the supernatural.

We cannot now stand on the metaphysics which the Christian world inherited from the Greeks, contrasting a 'real', eternal world of 'being' with a half-unreal process of 'becoming', for we do not establish contact with the 'real' by any repudiation of the contingent. We have to find what is 'real' in what is changing. Nor can we think, as some earlier generations thought, as though reality exists at two levels – the 'natural' going along by itself unless the 'supernatural' interferes with it. We must think in terms of a total, single environment to which man has to establish true adjustment, alike as organism and as spirit.

That total environment includes the ultimately mysterious, transcendent, yet self-disclosing and self-imparting Reality, self-subsistent, unqualified and unconditioned, on whom the whole structure of the world depends – for the 'natural' *presupposes* the 'supernatural' – the Reality which religion calls God. What is he like and what can we know about him? Christianity holds that God, who reveals himself in 'divers portions and divers manners' in all man's experience of life, is uniquely disclosed and communicated to us in a Life that shares the conditions of our humanity.

Christianity, as I have said already, is by its very nature 'supernatural'. It worships the infinite and transcendent God, who is not part of the world or contained within it; and its central conviction is that in Jesus Christ the Eternal, the Supernatural, the Transcendent penetrated the natural and historical to reveal himself and act in a human life. That is the mystery of the Incarnation. Any attempts to present Christianity in naturalistic or common-sense terms[1] will inevitably be presenting something else, which will in the end, be hardly distinguishable from secular Humanism with Christian overtones. It will not be a religion of redemption or good news of victory over sin and death.

A Christianity that is 'not mysterious' cannot support the weight of its own experience. But to say that is something very different from suggesting that Christians in the twentieth century can, or should try to, understand their religion in terms that are genuinely incompatible with such new knowledge as God may now be giving to us. Truth is one, and all truth is from the same Source. (That is implied by the great phrase in St. John, 'the true Light which lighteth every man'.)

In the present climate of opinion the word Supernatural is admittedly suspect. But when people reject 'supernaturalism' what they are rejecting – and rejecting rightly – is that crude, dualistic notion of a God 'interfering' with natural laws which we have inherited from the eighteenth century (Deism) but is now foreclosed by the scientific attitude; just as, when they talk about 'the death of God', what they really mean is the death of the traditional metaphysical system in which Christian belief has been, in the past, embodied, now badly shaken by philosophical criticism.

Christians must not interpret supernatural as meaning what is contrary to nature. Yet what the word stands for is a reality which is not the monopoly of Christian faith but disclosed in our own everyday experience. As it has recently been well said, 'the penetration of the natural by the eternal confronts us not only in the unique mystery of the Incarnation: it is involved in the daily commonplace mystery of Ourselves. If we were to recognize any straight cleavage between this and a wholly other

---

[1] As, for example, by Van Büren in *The Secular Meaning of the Gospel* (S.C.M.), where secular shades off into secular*ist*.

order of existence, it is indeed hard to be clear on which side man would fall.

'The divide between physics and metaphysics seems to run not between our own order and some remote uncharted mystery, but straight through ourselves and the content of our daily lives, even perhaps between sensory physiology and perception, or between "ourselves" and those external objects we call our bodies and brains. Whatever the relation between the this-worldly and the other-worldly, it can hardly be for integrated man a straightforward dualism.'[1]

Thus the fundamental question comes back, as in Christianity it always must, to the question about Jesus Christ himself. We have succeeded in making him into a 'problem', requiring defence and explanation, but he is offered to us as the Answer. The twentieth century question 'What is man?' is for Christians the question 'What think ye of Christ?' Who was he and what has he to say to us?

[1] From an article by Prof. John Morton (a biologist) in the *New Zealand Theological Review*, Vol. II, No. 1, p. 30.

2

JESUS THE CHRIST

CHRISTIANITY is an historical religion. It is not a system of doctrines and ideas or moral principles which can be recommended independently of their historical origin. It is rooted, or claims to be rooted, in things that happened, and above all in a life that was lived at one particular moment in history. The Gospel is proclaimed in the story of that life and death and resurrection, not in a set of abstract propositions. Indeed, one of my objects in this book is to show how the faith of Christianity flows out from the human life of Jesus of Nazareth; it is not something afterwards superimposed upon him.

Any new apprehension of the Christian world-view, any return to Christian faith and worship, depends upon a return to the Lord himself, with deeper commitment and fuller understanding. Thus, while history cannot itself create faith, Christian faith can never dispense with history or shirk historical investigation. One of the questions we shall have to ask, therefore, is how far the historical evidence is reliable and what is meant by 'the real Jesus of history'. Can we distinguish the Jesus of history (Jesus as he was) from the Christ of Christian faith, yesterday and today, the same for ever? Or is that an altogether false distinction? That question is bound up, as we shall see later, with the way we understand the New Testament and some knowledge of how the Gospels came to be written. That will come before us a little later on.

He lived in a world very different from ours. Jesus was a Jew of the first century and nothing can make him a twentieth-century man – if we try to do that we shall make a fictitious Christ. We live in a world which he could not have imagined, in which we are faced with all sorts of problems to which his teaching gives us no direct answer. His thought was conditioned, as any

15

real man's must be, by the presuppositions of his own time and by the Jewish tradition which he inherited. Can he still be for us the Way, the Truth and the Life? All *our* questions run back to that one.

Outward circumstances have changed immeasurably. The external conditions of life are very different from those that he and the first believers knew. But men and women are still men and women and their fundamental questions are still the same questions that life itself has put to them since the world began. Why are we here and where are we going? What essentially *is* a human being – a child of God and heir to eternal life created in the image of God and thus reflecting the purpose at the heart of things, or an accidental product of blind forces, washed up by chance on the beaches of evolution? What does human life ultimately *mean*? Is our environment for us or against us? Torn by our own interior contradictions and estranged as we men feel ourselves to be, where can we find that reconciliation which is the 'good news' of Christianity?[1]

It is to these 'unanswerable' questions that all the religious claim to provide an answer. These are what all the great Myths are about. These are what Christian theology is about – what 'God' means to man and what man means to God. But Christian theology is the age-long enterprise of interpreting what is *given* in Jesus Christ, and he gives the answer in himself, in the way he lived and the way he died. In St. John's Gospel he says 'I *am* the truth' (**14.** 6). If indeed he is, then what is implied in that? Can we still believe what our fathers believed about him? Can it be expressed in the same language?

There are many people in England who would say now that though they cannot accept Christianity as a 'supernatural' religion, they still acknowledge the Christian moral principles and respect what they call the ethics of Jesus. Can we not have the latter without the former? Is it not enough to honour Jesus as the teacher of a wonderful new morality but without the theo-

[1] 'To spread abroad thy Gospel, the glad tidings of reconciliation with thee.' (Office for the Consecration of Bishops in the Book of Common Prayer.)

logical mystifications? Is not all the rest unnecessary accretion which serves now only to hide from modern minds the great moral teacher and prophet of Galilee? Some Humanists indeed would go further than that. His ethical teaching, they would say, is still valid, but in what he taught or believed about 'God', that is, in his central personal convictions, he was living with the ideas of a past age and these are no longer possible for us. His ethics were right, his religion was mistaken.

The short answer to that is, quite bluntly, that there never was such a person as this simple moral teacher of Galilee. We shall look for him in vain in the New Testament – and no informed student can now suppose that there is any going back behind that. There is no pre-ecclesiastical source by which we can criticize or purge it. We can know Jesus only as the Church knew him; and that – to anticipate what must be said later – is what clearly emerges from all recent scholarship.[1] And the Church knew him not as a teacher of ethics but as the One who had brought God near to men. If we look at the teaching recorded in the Gospels, everything that he said about conduct was bound up with his belief in God and in man's relationship to God. If that was wrong, the ethical teaching was wrong – built on axioms that were in fact mistaken.

The suggestion now being heard in some quarters that he was the first atheist existentialist, who had 'the courage to be', to live and die, although he knew that there is no God, is a wanton outrage on all the evidence. It can be argued that his beliefs were wrong; what is incontrovertible is that he did hold them. We should come much nearer the truth in saying that he, in whom and through whom we believe in God, was himself the greatest of believers – 'the pioneer . . . of our faith', as *Hebrews* puts it (**12.** 2, *R.S.V.*).

The Christian faith of which he is the centre grows out of the faith which he himself professed and manifested in his life and

---

[1] I am reporting what the position is now, whether or not it is felt to be finally satisfactory. Whether this will prove to be the final position, in the sense of the last word of critical scholarship, is clearly a question that cannot be answered at present.

death – the religion of Christians out of his own religion. If he was wrong in what he believed about God and his own relationship to God, by which his whole activity was controlled, then he was in effect mentally deranged – as his own relatives seem at one time to have thought (Mark **3.** 21 and the following story). But delusions do not produce creativity. And here the great Schweitzer might be called as witness.

Schweitzer thought, and maintained in a famous book, that the whole outlook of Jesus was dominated by the expectation that at any moment, in the lifetime of those who were listening to him, 'before the standing crops had been gathered', God would intervene to bring history to an end and establish a new heaven and a new earth. 'The hammer of the world's clock was now raised to strike the last hour'. He died to make it come true – and it did not happen! But this Man who, according to Schweitzer's interpretation, died for a mistaken belief, laid his imperative, irresistible claim upon Schweitzer, calling him from a brilliant career with wealth and fame and honours at his feet, to that lonely hospital at Lambarene to devote his life to the service of lepers and sick primitive people for Christ's sake. The Lord's own ministry was reproduced in him.

An important part of the evidence for the truth of what our Lord himself believed and taught, and of what Christians came to believe about him, is the moral and spiritual creativity of the influence which has flowed forth from him through the operation of his living Spirit in the life and experience of countless Christians, and through them, directly or indirectly, in the lives of millions of people the world over who may have never so much as heard his name. That is fundamentally what the Resurrection means. The Resurrection seals his faith in God, as it creates Christian faith in him. By the Resurrection, as Peter said at Pentecost, 'God hath made him both Lord and Christ' (Acts **2.** 36).

Thus the teaching cannot be discussed as though it were separable from the Teacher. The teaching was preserved by the Church because it was his and because it reveals himself. Through it he communicates his own mind. And all the time it is forcing home upon us the question: 'Who do you say that I am?'

A. J. P. Taylor remarks in his recent volume[1] that during the period of the two world wars the Christian doctrine of the Incarnation came to be held by only a small minority, and that even for many professing Christians Jesus came to be regarded as the supremely Good Man but not more than that, not the Son of God in the theological sense. And this, he says, was 'as great a happening in English history as any since the conversion of the Anglo-Saxons to Christianity'. As to that, there is much that could be said. But it may well be that majority opinion at the present time does hold that he was 'just a man'.

Now *of course* Jesus Christ was a man, a real and intensely individual man. He was not a theological lay-figure or a god masquerading as human, or temporarily disguised in human form. That would make the whole story simply mythological, like one of the tales to be found in the Classical Dictionary. The New Testament writers have not the slightest doubt about that. There are even elaborate tables of his ancestry. His knowledge was limited as ours is limited. He was a man, who shared all our experience, sorrow and loneliness, hunger and thirst and fatigue. (During the storm on the lake, at the critical moment he had gone astern and was snatching a little sleep.) He prayed to God and he knew that he needed God's help. He was in the fullest sense a human person. And in this transitional period of theology the prevalent humanistic approach may prove to be marking the way to a new advance. For, even if one-sided or inadequate, it is the rediscovery of something essential and altogether indispensable for the Christian understanding of Christ himself and the Christian interpretation of human life.

Christian orthodoxy *requires* an unhesitating acceptance of his humanity, and Christians have too often been half-afraid of it.[2] Both in preaching and in popular devotion he has too long

---

[1] *English History 1914–1945* (O.U.P., 1965), p. 188.

[2] 'The nearer theology stays to the humanity of Jesus, the more relevant to the humanity of the receiver' – T. F. Torrance, *Theology in Reconstruction* (S.C.M., 1965), p. 26.

and too often been presented as a semi-real and half-human
figure such as one would never encounter in 'real life'. It was
rather like that when I was a boy myself. It would have been
thought 'irreverent' if not blasphemous to attribute normal
human reactions to him. (Younger Christians cannot begin to
realize the journey that our generation has had to travel.) 'I
have come,' he said, 'to set the world on fire' (Luke 12. 49). The
sentimentalized, effeminate figure portrayed in the Victorian
church windows and presented to us in sermons and 'divinity'
lessons was never in any danger of doing that! If the present
humanistic approach to Jesus has stripped him of these sub-
Christian disguises, that so far as it goes, is a solid gain. Yet
that is not all that there is to be said about it.

Certainly Jesus Christ was a man. But why does the world
still discuss and argue about him as it does about no other man
who has ever lived? What is the secret of his unique appeal?
Here very delicate insight is needed. For we cannot evade the
question 'Who is this?' The concrete meaning of Christian beliefs about him, the reality of what, as Christians hold, God has
done through him in the lives of men – that is, the Incarnation
and the Atonement – cannot be satisfactorily set forth in abstract theological propositions. It can only be significantly presented, as it always has been, in the Story. The Gospels are not
intended to be biographies, they are meant to proclaim 'the
Gospel' in a story (Mark 1. 1). We come to the story to learn
what it has to say to us, not to 'tell it' what it ought to have said.
We come to submit ourselves to the given, which is the properly
'scientific' attitude.

This does not, of course, mean an uncritical credulity, or an
abjuration of our rational faculties. We must use all the available
tools of criticism to find out what the story does say. Nor does
it mean an 'infallible' New Testament in the sense of one that
is verbally inerrant – it does not mean ceasing to be modern
men. But it does mean coming to it to let it speak to us, to
receive whatever it may have to reveal to us.

If we are to submit ourselves to the story, we must not begin
by scaling down the central figure in it to our own measure, or

cutting out as legendary accretions anything that we do not understand. Nothing could be more 'unscientific'. Our environment may be richer than we think it is, with depths in it which we have never realized. The world may be greater than we knew. There may be dimensions in it beyond ours. There may be more things in heaven and earth than are dreamed of in twentieth-century philosophy. We recognize freely that writers in the Bible were conditioned by their own time and circumstances. Let us not fail to remember that we, too, are conditioned by the climate of our own age, which can claim no monopoly of wisdom and certainly none of spiritual insight. As Jesus moves through the pages of the Gospels, a man among men, there is always something more, which seems to transcend the limits of our experience, something enigmatic, mysterious, magisterial, which seems to come, as it were from beyond, from some other and higher order of reality which yet, through him, comes into our world. In his own words, is it 'from heaven or of men'? What is it that he is communicating to us? What is it of which he appears to be the 'Mediator'? Mark's Gospel goes out of its way to emphasize how often the disciples who stood nearest to him 'could not understand' and 'were afraid to ask him' – and Mark does not mean merely that they were stupid. He was their trusted friend yet they stood in *awe* of him, and awe is an attitude very close to worship.

If we start from the human end, from where we are, and come to the Gospels in this way, experimentally, not with preconceived theological formulas – or with built-in emotional distrust of them – we shall find here an unveiling, a disclosure, of a quality higher than any we had conceived, of a transcendent spiritual Reality – Beauty and Holiness, Purity and Love – coming from beyond to challenge us and to redeem us, manifested in that human life. Then we shall be beginning to understand – though there may still be a long way to go – what was meant by the great Christian phrases: 'The Word was made flesh and dwelt among us'; 'This is true God and eternal life'. We shall be delivered, moreover, from that dualism which puts the questions we ask on a wrong footing, between Jesus of Nazareth 'as he really was' and Christ the Lord in whom Christians believe. 'He is not two, but one Christ.'

The Church did not turn a good man into a demi-god. It encountered the Presence of God in that good man. The meaning of life is seen in his living of it. The Divine is operative within the Human. Yet that must not be interpreted to mean, as our naturalistic bias would like it to mean, that what is best and highest in man *is* 'God', and that God is no more than man at his best and highest. That way we shall end by worshipping ourselves – the surest way to moral disintegration. 'God,' said the prophet, 'is God and not man', and on him we depend for our creaturely existence.

The God and Father of our Lord Jesus Christ – the God to whom Jesus taught men to pray – is the Creator of all the ends of the earth, without whom the whole universe would dissolve in nothingness. And therefore, to use extremely crude language, there is 'more' in God than can be revealed, and 'that' in his being which cannot be revealed, to the human mind or through a human life. How God is revealed to sub-human forms of life or to spirits other than man – if there be any such – it is beyond our power to conceive; we are men and can think only as men. But all of God that can be disclosed in man comes forth to meet us and claims us in Jesus Christ. That is what is meant by *calling* him 'Jesus Christ', at once and always both the Man of Nazareth and the source and centre of Christian faith in God.

For us, Jesus Christ is a proper name. We need to remember that for the first Christians it meant a tremendous affirmation of faith – that in Jesus God had come into their lives in hope and healing, forgiveness and renewal. The earliest band of 'Christians' were Jews, and they shared the Jewish Messianic hope. What distinguished them from the Jews was their conviction that they knew who the Messiah was and that he had appeared in the world already. The exciting, revolutionary gospel delivered by the Apostles at Pentecost, was that 'the Messiah is Jesus' – that this man whom they knew and all their hearers knew about, whom the priests had made Pilate crucify, was the Lord and the fulfilment of history, the bearer of God's redemptive purpose and the final word in the lives of men and women. The whole human situation had been changed. Something new had come into the world. This seemed to them to be so utterly urgent that they proclaimed it and called men to believe in it. In terms of the rather 'primitive' theology preserved in the early chapters of *Acts*, he had been *made* Christ by the Resurrection (Acts **2**. 22–36, but also, apparently, Romans **1**. 4).

It was the experience of the Resurrection, as verified in the Fellowship of the Spirit, which showed them who Jesus of Nazareth really was. He was the object of Christian loyalty, before any of the stories were told or written, and it was about him that they were told and thought to be important enough to be worth telling. There is no other Christ with whom we can make contact than the Christ of Christian faith and experience. This 'one Lord Jesus Christ' in whom we believe *is* the 'real Jesus of history', the man who has turned the world upside down.

Thus 'the two questions, Who is Jesus Christ? and Who was Jesus Christ? must be answered together, for the term Jesus Christ itself denotes Jesus of Nazareth as the object of faith and is, as such, in accordance with the presentation in the Gospels of Jesus as the Christ. The figure of Jesus appears in the Gospels both in his historicity and as the object of faith.'[1]

But why did they, how could they, come to think thus about him and to worship Jesus as Lord? Because, as we have hinted already, of the impression which he had upon them in the days of his flesh, what they had found in him, and what, through him, had found them. They believed that he was the Christ because he was that man, because he was Jesus. What manner of man, then, had he been? What was he like? How much can we know about him? Are the Gospels trustworthy documents? Or is this one more case of a mass of legends gathering round the founders of religions?

If we are not to be at the mercy of people who tell us that it is 'all bunk' and that Christian faith is founded on fiction, we must have at least some elementary knowledge of the way in which the New Testament took shape and of how the Gospels

[1] Article by Mark Glasswell in *Theology*, December 1965, pp. 558–63.

came to be written. The most recent developments in criticism have led some scholars to an extreme scepticism about the historical value of the Gospels. I shall argue that they give grounds for reasoned confidence.

3

THE SOURCES

THERE are probably few sane people left today who would argue, as many did in the nineteenth century, under the heady influence of *The Golden Bough* and other pioneer works of anthropology, that Jesus Christ never existed and is simply a creation of a 'Christ-myth'. Ronald Knox once 'proved' by the same method of argument that there never was such a person as Napoleon, or some equally fantastic proposition. What would be the consequences of accepting that? If Napoleon never really existed, then the battle of Waterloo never really happened and, in the long run, the French Republic is no more than a figment of the imagination. The same would even hold for such an event as the First World War, in which many still living actually took part.

One ground for believing in any historical character or any alleged historical event is the consequences which have followed, and the total dislocation of subsequent history which would result from their elimination. Along those lines we might say, and say with truth, that the fundamental 'proof' that Jesus Christ was a real Person in history is the rise, and the present fact, of Christianity. If we tried to eliminate Christianity, then the last two thousand years of human history remain inexplicable. Without him Christianity is inexplicable. Jesus is part of the history of the world.

But in fact the whole notion of a Christ-myth can now safely be left in a museum for monuments of misplaced ingenuity. To say that is not to pre-judge the question whether and how far legendary elements may have found a place in the Christian writings or in traditional Christian beliefs – that must be honestly faced as we go along. But that he actually lived and died is as certain as any fact of history, and indeed better attested than many. The Roman historian Tacitus refers to him in connection with Nero's persecution of Christians and says he was executed by Pontius Pilate. Suetonius, in his *Life of Claudius Caesar*, mentions him in connection with Jewish riots, though he calls him 'Chrestus' (i.e. the Good). Pliny, reporting to Trajan from Bithynia, speaks of the Christians meeting for worship and 'singing hymns to Christ as to a God'. So too, the historian Josephus – a Jewish prisoner of war in Rome after the destruction of Jerusalem – speaks of James (the James of Acts **15.** 13) as the brother of Jesus who was called Christ. The Jewish Sanhedrin tractate in the *Mishnah* says that Jesus was 'hanged on the eve of Passover'. To be put to death, he must first have lived.

These extra-Christian sources have value just because they have no case to defend. The authors are simply stating 'facts' known to them and are not writing in any Christian interest. But though they attest that Jesus did live and die, they tell us no more than that bare, elementary fact. To know what he said and did, what he was like, how people reacted and what his followers thought about him, it is to Christian sources that we must go. How far can we trust them and what emerges from them?

If we ask what are the sources of Christian evidence, it may be that the first and most fundamental answer is that the permanent witness to Jesus Christ is that which the Church commemorates on All Saints Day – that is, the total experience of Christians in all times and places from that day to this, out of every nation and kindred and tongue, who have known him best, who have consecrated their lives to him and through whom there has been given to the world in manifold varieties of expression, signal manifestations of his Spirit. Men and women so different and diverse, in origin, in temperament and culture, in the situations in which they had to live, in all traditions and affiliations, they have yet all of them, each in his own selfhood, shown forth some authentic reflection of his character. In many tongues they speak with the same voice, and in multiform actions and interpretations – St. Paul and St. John, Francis and Dominic – bear record to the same experience.

I asked them whence their victory came;
They, with united breath
Ascribed their conquest to the Lamb
Their triumph to his death.

But the primary evidence is, of course, the New Testament. Without the New Testament there would be no Church and without the Church there would be no New Testament. The two are correlative and complementary. For the New Testament, like the Old, has grown out of the life of the community, the worshipping and believing community, which in turn it helped to create and to sustain. It is primarily addressed to that community and should be approached not simply as a record but as the mediation of Christian experience nearest the source, at its greater depth and intensity. That is why it must always be authoritative, why the Church is always under its judgement, and why all the developments of Christianity as a living and growing movement in history must always refer to it for their verification.

This must not, of course, be taken to mean that we must do only what the first believers did or that Christianity ought to be tied forever to the patterns and practices of the primitive Church – Jesus himself says, in the fourth Gospel, that there is very much more to be learnt yet and that his Spirit will guide us into all truth. Christianity itself is still 'primitive' – two thousand years is a small space on the world's clock – and has to grow up into the fullness of Christ. It is not a static thing, it is creative, and it is not yet revealed what it shall be. No man can foretell what it may yet become. But the test of any new insights or developments is their truth to what is given in the New Testament. Nothing can be a genuine move forward, as opposed to a deviation or a cul-de-sac, if it contradicts the Scriptural faith and experience.

What has to be grasped, if we are to understand what the New Testament tells us about Jesus, and especially if we want to decide the question how far the Gospel records are to be trusted and whether we can find the 'real Jesus' in them, is how and why these writings took shape and what the needs which they were designed to satisfy. We cannot do that without making an excursion into the field of New Testament scholarship, however amateurish it may be – for I write as a student, not as a professor – conducted at such a pace and on such contours as will not defeat the beginner who has no familiarity with the subject.

There is at the moment a kind of iron curtain between the work of professional theologians, who are often blamed for being 'academic' (though as that is their Christian vocation, I do not know why) and the 'ordinary' Christian in the pew. There is need for more theological middlemen who can interpret the former to the latter and popularize academic findings in their relevance to Christian thought and life. For the man in the pew, and still more the man in the street, has a vague, demoralizing idea that something has happened in the Universities which makes the traditional Christian faith incredible but that the clergy are keeping it back from him. (How many people said that the Bishop of Woolwich had let the cat out of the bag at last!) But in fact there is nothing whatever to be afraid of. So long as we do not want to ascribe a literalist and verbal infallibility to the Bible as though it were a kind of celestial dictaphone, we shall find ourselves offered a stronger and clearer light for our understanding both of the New Testament – and within it, particularly of the Gospels – and of Christianity itself.

And we shall, I hope, find something more. We shall find how indiscerptible is the bond between Jesus of Nazareth and the Christian faith and between the Christian faith and Jesus of Nazareth. Let me therefore attempt to present the main results of recent work in New Testament criticism, and then make some attempt at an assessment of them from the point of view of what they may have to tell us about the reliability of the Gospels. Then we shall be able to go on and examine the story as the Gospels tell it.

*   *   *

It was thirty-five years after the Crucifixion before the earliest Gospel (Mark) was written, another fifteen to twenty-five before the publication of Matthew and Luke, and perhaps another ten before John appeared. The question is, what had been happening in the meantime, and why, in the end, did they take the form they did? Does the gap in time between the events and sayings recorded in the Gospels and their occurrence mean that the interval had been filled with the growth of theological speculations and mythological interpretations (largely coloured by Hellenistic influences) which so changed the original facts of the case by making Jesus into a Greek Saviour-God or a man from heaven, a celestial being, as to render the Gospels essentially unhistorical, products of Christian faith and imagination rather than factual and objective records?

That is what critics were saying not so long ago. Have we got to accept that negative conclusion? For if so, there seems to be little hope of finding the Jesus of history in the Gospel stories. But there is nowhere else that we can look for him. There is no going back behind the Gospels. There is nothing in writing outside the New Testament by which they can be verified or corrected. What then becomes of the claim that Christianity is in itself a historical religion, not a myth like the ancient nature worships?

On these four little books for nearly two thousand years the faith of millions of Christians has been nurtured and has brought forth the fruit of the Spirit of Christ. By them they have lived and with them they have died. In them they have found their Lord and Saviour. Through them they have been given a faith to live by and a victory that has overcome the world. Can all this wealth of spiritual experience be derived from a figure of Christian imagination, and not from Jesus Christ as he was and is? No Christian is going to accept that. Not merely because to accept it would be painful – we must not reject a conclusion on those grounds: we must ask What is true? not What should we like to believe? – but because we know already too much to accept a conclusion that would contradict the central certainties of our own experience. That conclusion, we know, must be wrong.

We must therefore take another look at the premises. Has

there not been too much begging of the question? Has it not been to lightly assumed that the interval between the original events in Palestine and the time when the Gospels were written and officially approved by the Church must have been filled by undisciplined myth-making? Is it not more reasonable to assume that the memories of actual eye-witnesses, like the Apostles who first proclaimed the Gospel, must have exercised some control, especially when it is recognized that the Apostles held a uniquely authoritative position, and were the organic centres of the community?

They had known Jesus and talked to him and lived with him, they had given up lives and livelihood to follow him, they had been his intimate and trusted friends, and it was to him that they owed their souls. Would they not have regarded those memories as sacred? Would they not have resented *and proscribed* any stories that might be put about which misrepresented the man whom they had known?

St. Paul, it is true, was not one of the Twelve, and he claimed to stand for a distinctive 'gospel' which he would allow nobody to tamper with under pain of excommunication (Galatians **1.** 6–9). He said it owed nothing to any human agency and had come to him by direct revelation. (Yet he speaks elsewhere of the heart of the Gospel itself as something that he had 're-ceived', that had been transmitted to him. 1 Corinthians **15.** 3.) He may never have seen or heard Jesus – there is no evidence either way for that. But in all his letters he shows himself acquainted with some of the seminal teaching of our Lord as afterwards written down by the evangelists, and he quotes one precious and characteristic saying of which there is no record elsewhere, 'It is more blessed to give than to receive' (Acts **20.** 35).

St. Paul, too, had stayed with St. Peter for fifteen days as his guest at Jerusalem (Galatians **1.** 18). Did they spend the fort-night talking about the weather? It seems to be certain enough that St. Paul, for all his theological developments and in spite of his disavowal of knowing Jesus 'after the flesh' (2 Corinthians **5.** 16) – which probably means 'as a *merely* historical figure' –

was closely in touch with the events as the first believers lovingly remembered them. Indeed, as I shall try to show later, we could deduce a sufficiently good idea of the kind of man Jesus had been from St. Paul's letters and other New Testament books even if we did not possess the Gospels.

The Gospels are not free compositions – the authors are not 'making up' the story – nor are they independent compositions. Any reader can see that the first three Gospels are very closely related to one another. Although there are sayings and incidents in all of them which are not found in any of the others, yet there is a great deal that they all have in common and for which they are drawing on some common source. They are dealing with traditional material which was already in circulation somewhere and derived, in the end, from first-generation eye-witnesses (Luke **1.** 2) but they are not dealing with it independently.

There is some interrelation between them and they seem to be using some common written document(s). That is the hypothesis which has been found necessary to explain both their agreements and their differences; and the view which is now generally accepted is that Matthew and Luke are dependent on Mark – almost the whole of which is contained in them – and on at least one other written document which contained a collection of parables and sayings as well as a certain amount of other material. That, of course, no longer exists, but Mark does. Mark is therefore a fundamental document for studying the Gospels in their present form.

A summary of the accepted position in what is called the documentary criticism of the Synoptic Gospels in written form will be presented later on in this chapter. It has long been known that documentary criticism can throw a great deal of light on the Gospel stories and can provide very useful tools for checking and assessing them where they differ. But the question remains, what lies behind them? How far can we trust the traditional material out of which the Gospels were composed? How did it come to take the shape it did and in what form did the evangelists have access to it?

It is here that a great deal of new work has been done (it is commonly known as Form-criticism) which has led to intensive critical debate, the result of which, in its first impact, was to reduce some important scholars to an almost totally sceptical position about the reliability of the Gospels as evidence for 'Jesus as he really was'.[1]

Form-criticism involves a highly technical and extremely elaborate investigation and no summary popular statement can do justice to it. What it involves, in principle, is the analysis of the structural forms in the various sections of narrative comprised in the Gospels as we have them, and then the attempts to trace them back to their origins in the life and teaching of the various churches founded by the apostolic missionaries. This means that the 'form' in which they are presented had been already worked into that pattern before it came into the hands of the evangelists, who were working, therefore, not just on floating material but on prefabricated blocks or units (*pericopae*) which they then composed, as best they could, into a continuous, running narrative.

Thus the order in which incidents occur does not represent their chronological sequence, as to which no information was available, but is no more than a guess by the evangelist or decided by quite other considerations. The Gospels are not chronological 'lives' of Jesus. The material in the Sermon on the Mount which Matthew works up into a finished sermon is found in Luke in a number of different places and is arranged in a number of different contexts. This is only one very obvious illustration.[2] But it means also much more than that. It means that the actual content of these passages has been already used by the Christian teachers, selected, shaped and interpreted in their sermons, in the light of the needs, interests and

[1] See, the quotations in W. Neil, *The Life and Teaching of Jesus* (Hodder) p. 11.

[2] Papias (early second century) says that Mark wrote down what he had learned from Peter 'accurately but not in order'. Dodd thinks that there was a traditional framework or order of which traces can still be found in Mark, although in fact he himself disrupted it. C. H. Dodd, *Historical Tradition in the Fourth Gospel* (C.U.P., 1963), pp. 233, 234.

circumstances – very widely different as these were – of the local Christian communities to which they were originally addressed.

It follows that the key to the understanding of a story or group of sayings in the Gospels is to trace them back, so far as we are able, to their setting in the life-situation of the church which had cast them into that form and ask what they meant to that circle of believers.

All this can sound highly disconcerting. Radical conclusions can be and have been drawn from it. From this position it is but a short step to saying that while the Gospels as we have them give us much reliable information about the life of the Church in the Roman Empire, they tell us little of true historical value about what happened in Palestine under Tiberius – much about the history of the Church, next to nothing about the history of its Founder, which must now be regarded as well-nigh irrecoverable.

That was how it seemed at first impact, though there are already movements of reaction towards a less paradoxical position. English scholars tended to wish it were otherwise, Germans on the whole welcomed it as a good thing or said that it does not matter at all anyway. It makes no difference to Christian faith; it rescues it from its mythological prison. The most thorough-going among them is Bultmann, who approaches the Gospels as an existentialist, for whom faith has little connection with history. What Bultmann means by his famous 'de-mythologizing' is taking Jesus out of the Christian 'myth' – death for our sins, resurrection, Ascension and coming again – in the framework of a three-storeyed universe, by which he is set forth in the New Testament.

How much then would be left? Almost nothing. But no matter, because for Bultmann the details of the earthly life are of small importance to Christian faith, if not indeed irrelevant.[1] (Barth came near to saying the same thing.) For faith is not

[1] Tillich refers to the lack of interest on the part of Japanese Buddhist priests in the earthly life of Gotama (*Ultimate Concern*, S.C.M., 1965, p. 141). But this is just where there is or should be a distinctive and characteristic difference. Christianity *must* take historical facts seriously.

tied to historical events. It consists in an existential decision when we are confronted by God and challenged to stake our souls on a commitment; and we are so confronted in the Christ of faith.

As Bultmann thinks that the Resurrection is 'mythical', in the popular sense of a fairy tale or legend, in other words that it never really happened, we may find it difficult to understand how he can believe in a Christ of faith at all. His faith is surely magnificent in its courage. Yet it has to be said right out that such an attitude is a break with the whole Christian tradition. It is in the very nature of Christianity that its faith rests on historical events, and on *these* historical events – the life and death and resurrection of Jesus – as the self-revealing activity of God. That faith would be dangerously shaken if its foundations in history were shaken.

Are we really being driven to that conclusion? When we reflect that the Church which believed in Christ exalted at the right hand of the Father, the Son of God, conceived by the Holy Ghost, fixed into its baptismal creed the 'crude actuality'[1] of the facts that he was crucified, dead and buried, is it likely to have remained unconcerned with preserving a trustworthy record of the facts – of what had been said and done by Jesus of Nazareth in his life on *earth* before the Crucifixion? All the probabilities are against it. And indeed a good deal of the evidence is against it.

It is not enough to be told that 'something' happened which led the first Christians to believe. Christians believe in God through Jesus Christ. What we want to be told is what did happen, through what words and deeds was that Man disclosed through whom God has disclosed himself to men? After all, Christianity is not something about our feelings or our religious attitudes. Christianity is something about God. If we know so little what Jesus himself was like, how can we say, as St. John's Gospel does say, that he who has seen him has seen the Father? It can hardly be doubted that the Gospels do at least profess

[1] On the whole question see C. H. Dodd, *History and the Gospel* (Nisbet, 1938, now in Hodder & Stoughton paperback).

to be telling us what did happen. Because they believed in Christ as the Church believed in him, are the facts distorted by their interpretation, so that we cannot rely on their objectivity?

The demand for purely 'objective' facts in history, just facts without interpretations (what is sometimes called scientific history) is asking for something which cannot be had. Uninterpreted facts cannot be made into history or invested with any historical significance. The historian has to interpret the data presented to him.[1]

For that matter, any scientific experiment involves a high degree of interpretation, and so does 'What I have seen with my own eyes'. When I 'see' a cat sitting on a mat my mind has coordinated and interpreted a bombardment of wave-lengths and sense-impressions, making them into the 'object' that I see. Until that has been done, I shall not 'see' anything. The cat, so to put it, will not be a 'fact'. The historian has to interpret his data, and neither can he, any more than the scientist, approach his data without presuppositions. Every historian has his point of view, and must start, like the scientist, from some act of faith. He must have some idea what he is trying to find and some faith that there is something to be found.

But what is that something? The facts are not just objects which can be picked up, arranged and classified and brought under generalized 'laws', for historical events are all unique. The life of Christ was indisputably unique; it can never, therefore, be laid down *a priori* that this or that 'could' or 'could not' have happened. We have to accept the 'given'; what *did* happen? But further than that, the facts of history are not just all the things that have happened – for millions of things happen every day of which there is neither memory nor record – they have always a psychological context. They are those in which people have been sufficiently interested, in which they have been deeply

[1] On this see James Peter, *Finding the Historical Jesus* (Collins, 1965) and Alan Richardson's Bampton Lectures, *History, Sacred and Profane* (S.C.M., 1963) and H. Butterfield, *Christianity and History* (G. Bell & Sons, 1949).

enough 'involved', by which their emotions have been so far aroused (whether by way of attraction or repulsion) as to secure their preservation in memory or tradition, if not in documents.

The reaction or response of the people concerned to the situation with which they were confronted – in the case now before us, their 'faith' – is part of the total historical event. The way in which people understood or interpreted, or what they thought and did as a result of things that happened *are* the facts of history. (An earthquake that nobody knew about or by which no human interests were engaged, would hardly be a historical fact at all.)

What all this seems to amount to is that records do not cease to be factual or 'objective' just because people have been interested, or even had 'interests', in what is recorded. Due allowance must no doubt be made for it, but the personal factor can never be eliminated, either from the historical data, the 'facts', or from the mind of the historian seeking to ascertain what the facts were. The historian has to identify himself, so far as he may, with whatever sympathy and imagination he may possess, with the hopes and fears and motives of those who were involved in the situation.

A completely detached attitude is impossible, or, if possible, is no positive qualification. If, like Gibbon or Bury, for example, the historian is congenitally allergic to the faith evoked by the events from Christians, he will make very little of Christian history. On the other hand, he will not be a worse historian if, given technical expertise and a conscience, he is writing himself from within that faith. And that is how the evangelists were writing.

The Gospels were written by Christians for Christians. As St. John states frankly in his *coda*, 'these things are written that ye might believe that Jesus is the Christ the Son of God, and that believing ye might have life through his name' (John **20.** 31). Does that mean that they are unreliable as evidence for what 'really happened', as delivered by those who from the beginning were eye-witnesses and ministers of the word (Luke **1.** 3)? How was that 'deliverance', that tradition, formed?

It is easy enough by slipping in words like 'folk-lore' to create the suggestion that the primitive Church became a kind of free-enterprise legend-factory in the supposed interests of faith. But folk-lore is an entirely false analogy. The believers were not pre-literate tribesmen. They lived in a highly sophisticated culture. Not all, not many of them perhaps, could read – St. Paul's letters were meant to be read aloud (Colossians **4.** 16); but those letters demand from their hearers a standard of intellectual receptivity which few preachers in twentieth-century England can expect to find in their congregations – who protest that the Epistles are 'unintelligible'. These people were not in the folk-lore stage at all. In any case, folk-lore is not just 'made up'. What it is, rather, is tribal tradition, like the patriarchal sagas in Genesis, memorized and verbally transmitted, and jealously guarded by the elders. Thus far the analogy might hold. But it must not be used to impute a *suggestio falsi*.

* * *

Mark opens his book with the words 'the beginning of the Gospel of Jesus Christ' – that is, the story which he is about to relate. The Gospel was proclaimed in the story. The New Testament taken as a whole makes clear that the apostolic proclamation, the *Kerugma*, the preaching of the Gospel, was delivered in the form of a presentation of the facts about Jesus Christ himself, and centrally, his death and resurrection (1 Corinthians **15.** 12), as guaranteed by eye-witness evidence (Acts **1.** 21, 22). Therefore the first need of the Christian missionaries, and of the converts who were gathered into the little 'churches' in Rome, in Corinth, in Ephesus, was to be taught, and trained to pass on, what was known about his days on earth by those who had actually been with him, 'beginning from the baptism of John until the day that he was taken up'.

These memories were authoritative and sacrosanct, to be reverently received and kept inviolable; for they were the fundamental Christian realities without which there was no Gospel to preach. These would have been entrusted to chosen men, solemnly committed to memory in the well-known usage of the

Middle East, drawn upon both for missionary preaching and
for the pastoral care of the congregations, and in turn transmitted to successors. (The original meaning of apostolic succession was guardianship of the purity of the tradition.)

This was how the tradition began to be formed and it seems
as though from a quite early date some of it at least got put
down in writing; for example, the Passion-story in the Gospels,
so solemn and quasi-liturgical in form, reads as though it existed already as a literary composition before being included
in the narrative; so the liturgical formula for the Eucharist (1
Corinthians **11.** 23–25) is commonly held to be drawn from a
written document. It goes back, St. Paul insists, to the Lord
himself.

The Epistles, the missionary correspondence – the earliest
Christian documents we possess – are richly coloured by actual
reminiscence of what Jesus was 'like', what he had said and
done. The descriptions of those qualities of spirit which ought
to be characteristic of Christians go back again and again to
the Lord himself. Peter had said in an early mission-sermon
that he had been anointed with the Holy Spirit (i.e., in Baptism) and that he went about doing good and healing all that
were oppressed of the devil, for God was with him (Acts **10.** 38.
Note that this summary is called 'the thing spoken', i.e. the
kerugma, the Gospel). Christians ought to be fashioned in his
likeness. 'Let this mind be in you,' St. Paul wrote, 'which was
also in Christ Jesus who . . . took the form of a servant (cf.
Mark **10.** 45; Luke **22.** 27, etc.) and in his human life (being
found in fashion as a man) humbled himself, becoming obedient
even unto death' (Philippians **2.** 5ff.). The Corinthians 'know'
– they have been told already – how for their sakes he became
poor that by his poverty they might be made rich (2 Corinthians
8. 9; cf. **6.** 10). He was one who 'pleased not himself' (Romans
15. 3) and Christians ought to think first of their neighbours, in
honour preferring one another, each considering the other man
higher than himself. To love one's neighbour is to fulfil the law:
Christians ought therefore to bless their persecutors (Romans
12. 14), never to render evil for evil, not to judge or to go to law

with one another (Romans **12–14; **1 Corinthians **6.** 7) but rather
to live in peace with one another, forgiving one another as God
in Christ forgave us (Ephesians **4.** 32).

All these injunctions (and many more could be quoted) are
earlier by some ten years than Mark, but they are quite clearly
dependent on sayings which were afterwards written down in
the Sermon on the Mount and elsewhere. St. Paul's account of
the fruit of the Spirit, the character which reflects the new life,
is surely meant to describe the Christ-character, and the hymn
of *Agape* (1 Corinthians **13**) which is the completed sketch, is
recognizably a word-portrait of the Lord himself – a portrait
which is validated and reproduced feature by feature in the Gospels (e.g. Philippians **4.** 6=Matthew **6.** 25).

If we go beyond St. Paul to other letters to the young Churches, we find just the same thing. It is better, says Peter, to
suffer for doing well than for doing evil, 'because Christ also
suffered for you (*R.V.*) leaving you an example that you should
follow in his steps: who did no sin, neither was guile found in
his mouth: who when he was reviled, reviled not again, when
he suffered, threatened not' (1 Peter **2.** 20ff). I do not discuss
authorship here. The ascription to Peter himself can be strongly
defended. So can other views! But it makes no difference to
our present point either way. 'All of you gird yourselves with
(a towel of) humility, to serve one another' (**5.** 5). Would that
have been said had it not been for the foot-washing? (*R.V.* mar-
gin accepts the reference to John **13.** 4, 5, 14). The unidentified
author of 2 Peter protests that his teaching about the 'Parousia'
was not a 'cunningly devised fable' but was based on eye-witness
of the Transfiguration (**1.** 16–18).

The Pastorals refer to a saying afterwards recorded in the
fourth Gospel (1 Timothy **2.** 5; John **3.** 17) and to the 'confession' before Pilate (1 Timothy **6.** 13) as well as two extracts from
early Christian hymns (**3.** 16 and 2 Timothy **2.** 11, 12). They
also supply evidence of the care which was taken to hand on the
tradition accurately (2 Timothy **2.** 2). And even in the Apocalypse there are echoes (e.g., the repeated 'He that hath an ear
let him hear' . . . and the day of the Son of Man as a thief

(Revelations **3**. 3; 1 Thessalonians **5**. 2; Matthew **24**. 43) – there are probably others.

The most 'academic' of the New Testament writers, the unidentified author of Hebrews, knows the Christ as the effulgence of the Father's glory and the true impress of God's being, seated at the right hand of the Majesty (**1**. 3). But he dwells lovingly and repeatedly on the characteristic facts in the life of Jesus, who was 'In all things like unto his brethren' (**2**. 17). He was one who had been made perfect through suffering. Tempted in all things as we ourselves are (cf. Luke **22**. 28) he is therefore able to help those who are tempted – a merciful and faithful High Priest (cf. John **17**) who had offered himself without spot to God. He had prayed 'with strong crying and tears' to God who was able to save him from death (**5**. 7) – surely a clear reference to Gethsemane – yet he learned the way of obedience and 'for the joy that was set before him endured the cross, despising the shame' (**12**. 2). What he was, that he is, what he is, that he was – yesterday and today the same and for ever (**13**. 8). He is at once the Christ whom the Church knew and the Jesus whom the Church remembered.

Thus the mission-preaching – the Gospel – involved all the time the preservation and transmission of what had really happened. But what, out of all the available material, was handed down to any particular Church-centre was clearly dependent on variable circumstances – on the special needs, or interests, or difficulties, in one and another local situation. The tradition was formed, in other words, through selection. The Epistles were not designed as formal treatises, they were *ad hoc* missionary letters addressed to particular local situations.

I should think it is likely – though this is merely a guess – that when one of these letters was recited (presumably when the Church was gathered for worship) the reader would illustrate and reinforce the Apostle's message by quoting examples of what the Lord had himself said or done, which would come to be treasured in that particular Church. In any case, there would always be local circumstances. Perhaps they were being hard-pressed by the Synagogue; how, then, had Jesus dealt with the

Jewish controversy? Perhaps there was persecution to be endured, but Jesus had given warning about that, and illustrative stories would be told, what he had said and how he had himself faced it, and these could hardly stop short of the Passion story. How ought we to pray? How can the sick be healed? We are told to 'love', but how did the Lord exhibit that? How can we overcome our fear of the demons? How do we know that our sins are forgiven? To these and a hundred questions of the same kind the answer would be extracts from the stories bearing on that situation.

Not every church would be placed in the same position, and they would not all be asking the same questions. Thus, although there was a common stock, the primary content of the *kerugma* itself, there would tend to grow up in the various church-centres different collections of stories, or at least collections differently arranged, as the special possessions of that particular church, and these would become the local 'tradition'. And these local cycles of tradition would have already definite 'shapes' of their own; either, at first, verbally memorized, or, as time went on, put into writing.

These 'shapes' or forms were the material out of which the Gospels were afterwards constructed. And that means that what we now read in the Gospels had been derived from the apostolic preaching based on the personal knowledge of disciples, carefully safeguarded in transmission, and had been already used and tested in the life and experience of believers before it came into the hands of the evangelists. It really does tell us about Jesus Christ and not only about early Church history.

The Gospel had to be preached and, as we have seen, the tradition became embodied in the preaching of it. But the converts, when made, needed pastoral shepherding, all manner of ethical problems had to be faced, and as the expectation of the Parousia began to recede into the background – contrast *Thessalonians* with *Ephesians* – the continuing life of the Church had to be organized. (We should notice, in passing, that the whole conception of a pastoral Ministry is of Christian origin and goes back to the Lord's own thought and practice as reflected in the discourse about the Good Shepherd [John 10] and the parables in Luke 15.)

For example, what about the Christian marriage laws? There was a definite saying on that, and St. Paul refers to it as authoritative in his own considered discussion of sexual ethics (1 Corinthians 7. 10). What about the ethics of money and property? Jesus had said many trenchant things about that, and those sayings could be collected and quoted and, to the best of their lights, 'applied'. Or again, how could Jewish and Gentile converts really share in the life of the community? This very early became a burning question (Galatians, especially 2. 2ff.; Acts 10. 15). What about the Sabbath? 'The Sabbath was made for man.' When that was quoted the teacher might introduce it by the story of what had led up to that saying: 'one day when he was going through the cornfields . . .' (Mark 2. 23ff.). What about the Jewish food law? Jesus had said that purity of heart, not ritual purity, was what mattered. Did that abrogate the Jewish food laws? (See the editorial comment at Mark 7. 19b.) What about the practice of fasting? or almsgiving? (Matthew 6). How far does love for the neighbour extend? (Matthew 5. 43; Luke 10. 25ff.). What ought to be the attitude of the Christians, as citizens, to the imperial government? What attitude had the Lord taken (Mark 12. 13ff. which clearly underlies Romans 13. 6; John 19. 2, and other passages).

To meet these and many other similar questions there came to be formed collections of sayings, some with introductory stories attached to them, and parables and other teaching material for the edification and training of Christian life. These collections might vary between one church and another – the church in the metropolis, for example, the *milieu* out of which Mark was written, would be likely to have problems rather different from those of the churches in Asia or Syria. But a common stock came to be accumulated and before long to be circulated in writing. (A little later, indeed we can almost trace it.) Thus side by side with the basic *kerugma*, the events by which the Gospel was constituted, there was growing up a tradition of

Teaching (*Didache*) to be handed down for the guidance of life in the Church.

This was formed from memories of the Lord's own words. But – and this must be faced – in process of transmission some of the sayings came, perhaps inevitably, to be reshaped and re-interpreted and sometimes even given a changed meaning, by being 'applied' to the life of the Church in the world under new conditions and in different circumstances. (*Any* attempt to for-mulate 'Christian Ethics' must always come to terms with that same difficulty, and the Church has to face it in every genera-tion.) Thus, to take one example, 'Agree with thine adversary quickly', originally a warning not to dither in facing the crisis of the Kingdom of God, becomes a general injunction not to neglect opportunities of reconciliation. In the Gospels them-selves, the Parable of the Sower is followed by a sermon about the parable (Mark **4.** 13–20 and parallels) in which it has been turned into an allegory and used to convey a meaning which seems to differ from the speaker's original intention.

We need not be shocked by this recognition. What any crea-tive genius 'means' – what Shakespeare 'meant', for example – is always more than he says in words at the time, more perhaps than he is himself aware of. One can say that the Christians read their own meanings into the dominical parables and say-ings and that this was an illegitimate thing to do and shakes our confidence in the records. But another way of putting it would be this. The sayings, received into their hearts and minds, were found to be speaking to their own condition. Through them Christ was speaking to his Church, not only to those who first heard them spoken.

What was their meaning, in terms of faith and obedience, for the Christian life-situation then and there? In every generation the Church must ask that. What Christians have found, or may yet find, in the Teaching may be truly said to be part of what it 'means'; and the Lord himself said that more would be found in it than he had been able to say in his time on earth (cf. John **16.** 12ff.). Yet as a check on undisciplined speculation and individualistic interpretation, we must always be going back, so far as we can, to what the Lord intended the words to mean in the situation in which they were first uttered. We must read new meanings out of them rather than into them. They must not be used to support our own ideas. These sayings are the remembered words of Jesus.

We can never be sure, in any particular instance, that what we read is a verbatim record. They come to the English reader through two translations. They may be preserved for us in variant forms, because they have come down through different channels, or through different editorial treatment or different renderings of the Aramaic. But some are so unmistakably characteristic that they could be recognized wherever we heard them. Of the rest we can have at least reasoned confidence that their general purport and tenor has been preserved for us, that they do truly reflect the 'mind of Christ'. The remembered words still echo in Christian hearts, as indeed they have echoed across the centuries in lands of which Jesus himself had never heard, speaking to men who are not called by his name, of hope and freedom, justice and world-brotherhood. Are these the words of a temporary visitant, long ago swept away by the tides of history? Are not these 'words of eternal life' (John **6.** 68)?

The Church lives by the memory of Jesus, which is the bond of its continuing life, as a nation, and still more a family, lives by its corporate and familiar memories. (Mrs. Smith has an historical existence. As a figure in history, historians, biologists, sociologists, psychologists, may do their best with her – or their worst. Only to her children is she 'mother'.)[1] The Jesus whom it remembers is its Lord, and its Lord is the Jesus whom it remembers. All this is set forth in its central act of worship. In the Eucharist, the two liturgical 'highlights' are the breaking of the Bread and the reading of the Gospel. The Church 'proclaims the Lord's death' (the thing done); it rehearses his remembered words (the things spoken), and partakes of the bread and wine in the presence of the Living Christ.

[1] John Knox: *The Church and the Reality of Christ* (Collins, 1963).

4

THE GOSPELS

WE have seen that there are two main streams of tradition – the proclaimed events – the Gospel – and the Teaching. The two streams meet in the Gospels as we have received them. What follows is probably known to the reader already, and if not can be found in any recent commentary. It need only be stated here in the barest outline.[1]

If the first three Gospels, the Synoptics, were printed out in three parallel columns and if we then underlined in one colour everything that occurs in all three, we should find that virtually the whole of Mark is contained in Matthew and/or Luke, and much of it in the same verbal form, though not in the same places or in the same order. Mark has in fact been incorporated, as a written document, into the other two. (Matthew depends more closely on him than Luke does.) Mark is therefore the fundamental document.

Now St. Mark, as we know, was a cousin of Barnabas; his mother had a house in Jerusalem; and he had been chaplain or A.D.C. to St. Paul on the first missionary journey (Colossians 4. 10; Acts 12. 12; 13. 5) and is subsequently found with St. Paul in Rome (Philemon 24). A statement from the early second century (Papias) which there is no reason to set aside, connects him very closely with Peter's dictation. (Form-criticism would put this rather differently.) He stood very close to eye-witness sources. His Gospel which, though it contains some teaching, consists mainly of narrative of events, represents the kerugmatic tradition as it had taken shape in Rome, i.e. in a church predominantly Gentile. (Jewish customs had to be explained, cf. Mark 7. 3ff.). It can be dated within very narrow limits – after the Neronian persecution and before the destruction of Jerusalem

[1] There is a good vivid summary in W. Neil (op. cit.) Ch. 3.

(A.D. 70) – suggesting a date about A.D. 65. It is written in very rough Greek indeed, with none of Luke's literary artistry, and has throughout a 'primitive' feel about it. It breathes in something like the original atmosphere.

If we now underlined in a different colour the material found both in Matthew and Luke other than that which they have drawn from Mark, we should find that they both contain much in common, mainly sayings and parables of Jesus, often in a form which is verbally identical, though inserted at different points in the narrative and sometimes very differently arranged. Where did this come from? Which copied the other? The answer now generally accepted is that both are using the same written document – one of those early collections of teaching-material to which reference has been made already (another was circulating in Egypt, and there are traces of it on papyrus-fragments). The collection which Matthew and Luke are using is commonly held to have been compiled in Antioch, the first centre of Gentile Christianity, and to have been already written in Greek – they transcribe directly, they did not have to translate it – and probably about A.D. 60 (for Mark himself seems to have had knowledge of it) when men still living could have heard the words spoken. The theological code-name for it is Q (from the German word *Quelle* = Source).

There will still be a good deal left with no colour markings. Matthew and Luke each have material – sayings, incidents and the Infancy stories – which is not to be found elsewhere in the Gospels. (In Luke it is a very substantial section and includes the Prodigal Son and the Good Samaritan.) For these they were drawing on sources of their own (labelled for convenience M and L) which it is not now possible to identify – though Luke had spent two years in Caesarea (Acts **24.** 27) and could have met some original disciples.[1]

Here, then, is the Four-Document hypothesis – Mark, Q, L

---

[1] Some hold that Luke had written his first draft ('proto-Luke') and subsequently came across Mark which he then inserted into his own document; but that would not affect the general position, except that Q would be definitely earlier than Mark, i.e. perhaps ± A.D. 60.

and M – which is now accepted almost universally as the origin of the Synoptic Gospels and shows how the tradition is embodied in them. It follows that what is found in all three of them has not more authority behind it than anything that is found in Mark alone; the main weight must always fall on Mark. On the other hand anything that is found both in Mark and in Q independently – comes, that is, from both streams in the tradition – will have the strongest possible attestation.

Luke, as we know, was Paul's personal doctor and so in very close touch with early sources. Himself a convert from the Gentile world, an educated Greek professional man with considerable literary gifts, he was an artist-historian, a humanist and (as befits St. Paul's travel-companion on the Gentile-mission) a universalist. When he wrote, Jerusalem had been destroyed and the Church was now predominantly Gentile. Luke–Acts is now generally dated somewhere about A.D. 85–90 when the first-generation believers would have been dead. But his sources, as we have seen, go back to within some thirty years of the Crucifixion.

The authorship of Matthew is unknown and the book is not at all easy to place. It was written in Greek, i.e. for a Gentile Church, yet it seems to represent a revulsion from the Pauline attitude to the Law towards a more Jewish and legal interpretation of the words of Christ as the Law of the Kingdom of God. (The Sermon on the Mount, for example.) St. Matthew, whoever he may have been, was essentially an ecclesiastic. His Gospel is probably to be dated about A.D. 90. It must be said that broadly, and in principle, material found in Matthew alone is the least reliable stratum in the Synoptics.

The fourth Gospel presents its own problems. It is written out of the heart of a mature faith and a developed Christian theology in which Jesus is the Son of God, in the full metaphysical meaning of the phrase – the eternal Word by whom all things were made, the only begotten, pre-existing Son who was 'in the bosom of the Father'. (Though the Synoptics do not go so far as that, there is in fact little in this development which is not already implicit in Q: Matthew **11.** 27; Luke **10.** 21, 22.)

Before Abraham existed he *was* eternally (John **8.** 58). He that
has seen him has seen the Father (**14.** 9). He is the bread of life
and the light of the world – the true light that lighteth every
man, and the incarnation of the being of God.

Clement (150–215) called it a 'spiritual Gospel', and all
Christian experience would agree with him.[1] The richest Christian devotion has been nurtured by the imagery of the Good
Shepherd, the great Discourse which precedes the Passion, the
wonderful story of the Easter Garden and the gift of the Lord's
forgiveness to Peter. It seems to bring us nearer the Christ whom
the Church knows than any other book in the New Testament.
Yet few raise questions more difficult than this does. The writer
is so concerned to interpret that the 'facts' seem to be all 'interpretations', overwhelming history altogether. How far can
St. John be regarded as really historical?

In recent years there has been a shift of opinion. When I was
a student, this book was the battleground between orthodoxy
and liberalism (or 'modernism'). For the former it was the very
ark of the covenant; orthodox belief was held to be bound up
with defending its factual reporting and its authorship by John
the son of Zebedee. It was treated indeed as the primary authority, directly dependent on eye-witness evidence,[2] more firmly
based on history than the other Gospels. Liberals took exactly
the opposite line. The author, they felt, could not have been a
Jew (despite such sayings as **4.** 22 – would a non-Jewish author
have laid stress on that?). The whole tone of the book is Hellenistic; it breathes in the air of Greek philosophical mysticism
(Dean Inge presented that case very persuasively), and it is a
re-translation of the Gospel from its original, Jewish presentation into the language and thought of the Greek world –
the bridge by which Christianity passed over to become a
universal religion. It is thus a work of theological genius,
or a profound Christian meditation, rather than a record of
what really happened. It was that opinion, or something

[1] Though Clement may have meant 'allegorical'.

[2] That claim is made, for one incident, in the book (**19.** 35), but we cannot assume that the writer is referring to himself. So also in **21.** 24.

not far from it, in which liberals of my generation grew up.

Now all the early references to this book are agreed that it was written in Ephesus, and its probable date is about the end of the century. (It cannot be much later than A.D. 100, since fragments of it have now been found on papyri which experts date at about 120.) Thus it took shape at a time and in a place in which the Church would be almost entirely Gentile, and Jewish Christianity nearly forgotten. It seems clear that the writer *was* strongly influenced by ideas in the current Hellenistic philosophy. Indeed the astonishing thing about him is how he grasps and fuses both the Hebraic and the Greek ways of thinking in one single mind. But C. H. Dodd has shown in a masterly treatment that, although the author is primarily an interpreter, there are yet throughout the fourth Gospel clear traces of an early Palestinian tradition, closely connected with Jerusalem and intimately acquainted with its topography (and therefore earlier than the Jewish revolt [A.D. 66] and the siege and destruction of the city) which are inseparably interwoven in it.

There is not space here for detailed illustrations – some will come before us as we go along. But this changes the whole situation. We need no longer be shut up with the question: Is John right or were the Synoptics right? They may be regarded, rather, as complementary. There may be points at which John can be used to amplify, or even correct, the earlier accounts.

Any reader can see, for example, that whereas, according to Mark, the Lord's ministry was exercised mainly in Galilee, leading up to the final journey to Jerusalem, and apparently occupied only one year, John represents it as centred in Judaea with occasional expeditions to Galilee, and, apparently, as occupying three years. But there is a good deal in the Synoptic narrative, not least in the events of the Passion week, which can be more readily understood if Jesus had been in the capital more often than the Marcan scheme apparently allows for. There are, too, not a few sayings in Mark and/or Q which are echoed, though in a different form, in John; and often it seems that it is he who gives us the true implication and meaning of the Lord's words,

D

even though he may not have spoken them quite like that. And again, though the reader sometimes feels that Jesus has been removed from the actual scene of history to a remote theological stratosphere, yet more than once John goes out of his way to emphasize his 'human' traits and emotions, and to make it clear that he is the Son of Man in the meaning which is now popularly attached to that phrase. (That he had no leanings towards 'docetism', playing down the Lord's real humanity, is clear from the warnings in the Epistles against those who deny his coming 'in the flesh', that is, in our psycho-physical human nature. This is the deceiver and the anti-Christ [1 John **4.** 3; 2 John 7]. Jesus is never a mere theological symbol.)

In sum, though we can no longer defend the literalism which was widely assumed even fifty years ago, it can now be taken that this haunting book stands much closer to the original forms of the common tradition – that is, to the events, to the deeds and words of Jesus of Nazareth – than liberal scholars had hitherto supposed.[1]

[1] See C. H. Dodd, *Historical tradition in the Fourth Gospel* (C.U.P. 1963) and Hoskyns and Davey, *The Fourth Gospel*, two vols. (Faber, 1940) and Alan Richardson's S.C.M. paperback, *St. John's Gospel.*

5

THE BACKGROUND

THE Old Testament cannot be rightly interpreted without at least some elementary knowledge of its geographical and historical background. The prophets were not uttering into the void, nor were they 'predicting' the far distant future. They were passing moral and religious judgements on the situations in which they and their hearers were involved; and these were largely due to the politics of the two great River-empires between which Palestine was a border-state. The reader must know something about all this if he is to understand the prophetic message. Similarly, to follow the story in the Gospels, we need to see the life and teaching of Jesus in the framework of the political situation as it was in contemporary Palestine. Indeed, one test of its historicity is that it does fit exactly into the facts known, from other sources, to have existed between about A.D. 26 and 36. Luke (3. 1) carefully gives the exact date (A.D. 29) and then the names of the leading political personalities when Jesus came forward on to the public stage to become part of the history of the world.

The important fact to remember is that Palestine was a country under Roman occupation, and was, unlike other more prosperous Provinces, a crater of smouldering resentments, erupting from time to time in futile risings against Roman 'imperialism' and its taxes (Acts 5. 36, 37). ('Publicans' were minor officials of the Revenue, employed by the imperial authorities, and therefore regarded as renegades and quislings. No holy man, and certainly no patriot, would eat and drink with publicans and sinners.) Popular Messianic expectation tended, therefore, to be fixated in liberationism. No one would be accepted as Messiah if he did not offer 'Independence Now'. Anyone who seemed to be offering hope of that would only too quickly have a mob

behind him. That was the kind of leader they would follow –
and what Jesus steadfastly refused to be. For this reason Messiah was a dangerous word, which might spark off an attempted
insurrection; and this may go some way to explain the repeated
injunction to silence in Mark's narrative and the apparent re-
luctance of Jesus to make public use of that title, as well as his
alarm at the threatened consequences after the feeding of the
five thousand.

This last point is brought out by the fourth Gospel. Mark
says that 'straightway' after the miracle Jesus compelled the
disciples to leave and sent them back to the other side of the
Lake (Mark **6.** 45). John makes clear what was the reason for
that; it was his fear of a mob-demonstration of which he would
forcibly be made the leader (**6.** 15). Similarly in John's account
of the Trial, where the priests appear before Pilate as prosecutors
and not simply to ask for official confirmation of an ecclesiastical sentence, the political implications are frankly stated.
(They would be highly embarrassing for Mark, writing in the
metropolis under Nero.) The whole trial turns on a claim to
kingship. Pilate had already found him not guilty, but the priests
persevered in the charge of treason. 'If you let him go you are
not Caesar's friend.'[1] It was as a king and potential rival to
Caesar (cf. Acts **17.** 7) that our Lord was condemned and executed (cf. the mocking 'title' over the Cross). Pilate, as Dodd
remarks, did not believe it, but it was the only charge on which
the sentence could be given any legal justification.

In occupied territory, as was seen in the last war, the population
becomes divided between the Resistance and Collaborationists,
and people would always be wanting to find out on which side
of the line Jesus stood: Is it lawful to give tribute to Caesar or
not? (The answer he gave to that was not merely evasive; he was
saying that God's sovereignty is absolute and must therefore

---

[1] What this means in our vernacular is 'You will lose your "K"'.
Friend of Caesar (Caesaris amicus) was an imperial title of honour. A
Prefect of Egypt had been removed from the roll for malpractices. Pilate,
who was in no favour with Rome, took the hint. But Pilate was too much
even for the Roman Colonial Office, and was eventually recalled and
exiled.

never be identified with the relative loyalties of politics.) But religion tends also, under these conditions, to be driven in upon itself – we have known how in war-time Christianity becomes almost equated with the national cause – and to become narrow and defensive; and too much religion, as Jesus encountered it, was hard, legalistic and defensive.[1]

The various sects and parties in Judaism were divided not only on religious matters ('the Sadducees did not believe in the Resurrection') but also by their attitudes to the Roman question. The Zealots, who were specially strong in Galilee and one of whom, Simon Zelotes, was included among the twelve, were 'cloak and dagger' men, intransigent nationalists, always working for violent rebellion. Memories of the Maccabean revolt led them to cherish false dreams of success. Jesus saw very clearly where it was leading and gave stern warnings of what the result must be. It could end only in ruin and destruction, with not one stone left upon another. Forty years later history proved him right, as the arch of Titus still bears witness.

The Sadducees, the high-priestly dynasty, who might perhaps be compared with our Whig bishops, depended upon the imperial authority for their status, their privileges and their emoluments. Any threat of a popular disturbance, any news of a claimant to Messiahship, would send a cold shiver down their spines. 'The Romans will come and take away both our place and nation' (John 11. 48). The Pharisees, the most friendly towards Jesus and the best elements in the Jewish Church – the most progressive and the most devoted – were the heirs of the Maccabean 'separatists' (1 Maccabees 2. 29, 42) and in principle, accordingly, anti-Roman – their left wing more strongly so than their right. They were therefore opposed to the vassal Herod princes. The so-called Herodians were their creatures.

When Jesus was born, the whole country was governed under

[1] It must be remembered, too, that the Roman Empire, especially in the Eastern province, was Hellenistic not Latin in culture. Consequently, as in the days of Antiochus Epiphanes, the pure Jewish tradition was constantly exposed to Hellenization – or, as we should put it now, secularization. The greater the danger of secularization, the more would the Church, like ours, tend to concentrate on its own institutional defences.

'indirect rule' by Herod the Great, a Jew by religion but in taste and sympathy a Hellenist, who fed his ambition to be a second Solomon by a grandiose and extravagant building programme, which he tried to finance by merciless taxation. He was cruel, crafty and generally detested. (Augustus remarked about him in a Greek pun which cannot be reproduced in English, 'I would rather be that man's swine than his son'.) On his death (4 B.C.) the country was divided into three petty sheikhdoms or 'tetrarchies' under his three sons, who appear in the Gospels, Archelaus, Antipas and Philip. Archelaus, who held Judaea, was a disaster and the people petitioned, in vain, for his deposition. (There may be a reference to this in the Parable of the Pounds in St. Luke **19.** 12, 14, 27.) When he was deposed (A.D. 6) Judaea was put directly under a Roman procurator, Pontius Pilate, the fifth in the succession, being appointed in A.D. 26. The Herod of the Ministry is Antipas – 'that jackal', as Jesus once referred to him – who ruled under Roman authority in Galilee and built the Greek capital at Tiberias. Once on the Eastern shore of the lake you were safely outside his jurisdiction, and this may account for some of our Lord's crossings.[1]

But outside these organized sects or parties there were the people who had not spoken yet – the 'meek', the 'quiet in the land', the quietists, taking no part in public affairs and controversies, practising a devout personal religion and 'looking for the consolation of Israel' (Luke **2.** 25, 30). 'Comfort ye, comfort ye my people saith your God.' Whatever the sources of information on which Luke relied for these early chapters, even if, as some hold, the great songs, or Canticles, are his own free composition, they do faithfully reflect the religious outlook of the circles out of which, it must be remembered, both John and

[1] Josephus says that Herod's arrest of John Baptist was due to fear of political agitation. Mark gives no hint of that and puts the whole blame on Herodias and Salome. Herod spoke of Jesus as John come back from the dead (i.e. to continue to plague me) but took no action against him. It is however significant to read that when Jesus was told about the execution he withdrew the disciples into a desert place (Matthew **14.** 12, 13).

Jesus himself came. This may throw light on what they themselves were to stand for. What we have here is not concern with nationalism nor apocalyptic visions of Judgement. The note is one of fulfilment and deliverance:

Through the tender mercy of our God
 Whereby the dayspring from on high has visited us,
To give light to them that sit in darkness and in the shadow of death
 And to guide our feet into the way of peace. (1. 78, 79)

Thus all in all, we can feel reasoned confidence that the Gospels do rest solidly on history. 'History did not cease to be history because it was interpreted. Mark gives us a patchwork of tradition; but on analysis every part of it bears witness, in its own way, to a "Jesus of History" behind it.'[1]

ADDITIONAL NOTE

For a recent and positive valuation of the historical quality of the Gospels, the reader is referred to Professor C. D. Moule's book, *The Phenomenon of the New Testament* (S.C.M., 1967) published while these pages were being printed. I venture to quote some short extracts, by kind permission of the S.C.M. Press, Ltd.

'Some not inconsiderable groups of scholars are daring once more in a sense to look back to the Jesus of history; but now they are finding, not the Liberal Protestant figure, but a figure as challenging, as supernatural, as divine, as is found on the hither side in the apostolic Gospel. The barrier between the Jesus of history and the Christ of faith is thinning, and the continuity increasing. Dare we speculate that, one of these days, they might even come to coincide?' (p. 47)

'Recent theological writing has tended to dismiss the importance of history in favour of the transcendental call to decision (e.g. Bultmann) or to dismiss the transcendent in favour of such history as may be comprised within the categories of purely human comprehension. But I cannot see how any serious student of Gospel origins can concur with either . . . On the one hand, the old Liberal Protestant way of stripping off the transcendental and rendering the Gospels rationalistically intelligible is widely agreed to have been a *cul-de-sac* . . . On the other hand, a Gospel which cares only for the apostolic proclamation . . . is really only a thinly-veiled Gnosticism or Docetism, and . . . will prove ultimately to be no Gospel' (p. 80).

---

[1] *Oxford Dictionary of the Christian Church*, on Mark.

6

THE FORERUNNER

AT the top of his page Mark sets the chapter-heading, 'The beginning of the gospel of Jesus Christ the Son of God.' What he intends by that we know already. The gospel is proclaimed in the story of the Lord's life and death and Resurrection, and this is how Mark is about to set it forth. The story began with the coming of John the Baptist – the whole tradition is constant on that. The Christians attached very high importance to it, for John had prepared the way of Christ before him. (For the evidential use that was made of John and his testimony in the early preaching see Acts **10**. 37; **11**. 16; **13**. 24, 25; **19**. 2–4.) John was the Messenger sent before his face (Malachi **3**. 1).

John's appearance had caused immense excitement and awakened intense popular expectations. For here was the revival of prophecy. Since the exile prophecy had been muted: 'There is no more any prophet, neither is there among us any that knoweth how long' (Psalm **74**. 9). But there was a belief that it would be reborn (see 1 Maccabees **4**. 44–46); that a great prophetic figure would arise – perhaps a Moses (Deuteronomy **18**. 18), perhaps an Elijah (Malachi **4**. 5) – and that this would be a sign that the Day of the Lord, the promised day of deliverance, was dawning. And when John, like the prophets of old, came out of the desert with his message of repentance and cleansing – a baptism of repentance unto remission of sins – that expectation seemed to have come true. He seemed like Elijah *redivivus*, in dress, in manner of life, in moral stature, confronting Antipas and his paramour as Elijah had Ahab and his Jezebel. He had come, surely, as the promised Messenger. Could he be even more than that, the Messiah? (John **1**. 19).

John took no such exalted view of himself. It was Jesus who called him the Elijah (Mark **9**. 13) and more than 'a' prophet, *the* prophet, the forerunner (Matthew **11.** 9, 10; Luke **7.** 26, 27). John disclaimed any status in his own right. It doesn't matter, he said in effect, who I am; I am simply a voice, preparing the way of the Lord (Isaiah **40.** 3). His commission was to point away from himself to a greater than he who was to follow, to bring to fulfilment the work he had begun. It is some measure of that moral grandeur, to which Jesus paid such high tribute – he called him the greatest man born till then – that, leading a nation-wide religious movement, when he might have become a great national figure and had the population at his feet, he subordinated himself to his successor. His water-baptism was but the first stage towards that baptism with the Spirit which would be the inauguration of the new age (Joel **2.** 28ff.; Acts **2.** 14ff.). Christianity is the heir to John's mission.

Jesus regarded John with reverence – it was he to whom, under God, he owed his calling. Yet he insisted that with his own coming a new age had begun – an age no longer of prophecy and expectant preparation but of fulfilment. History had, as it were, started again; and as John had stood on the other side of the line, 'he that is least in the kingdom of heaven is greater than he' (Matthew **11.** 11). With Jesus himself the promises were realized.

John's message was that of Elijah and the great prophets. It is no good saying Abraham is our Father. God is not dependent on Israel. The day of the Lord need not be the day of Israel, it may be her defeat and humiliation. The day of the Lord may be darkness and not light (Amos **5.** 18), and it will be, if the nation remains faithless. Neither birth nor inheritance will save you, only a change of heart and obedience. So there must be a radical reformation, with the axe laid to the root of the trees; and John summoned the people to take part in a national mission of repentance and hope.

In Mark and Matthew John is represented, as he is still in Christian imagination, as primarily a prophet of doom, by contrast with the 'gospel' of Jesus. 'His was not good news, it was bad news.' It is not at all certain, however, that this is the whole truth. He uttered stern warnings about the Judgement and he compared his hearers to adders scuttling away before a bush fire. But every disclosure of God in history, like any great work of art or any important moral issue, must involve a sifting, a separation, a judgement. Men take sides one way or the other; they are judged by it and lay themselves bare by their response, by the attitude they adopt, as Jesus himself frequently insisted. ('Don't know' or 'Couldn't care less' may imply a judgement as well as 'Yes' or 'No'.) The wheat will be separated from the tares, the useless fish in the net will be thrown away, the first shall be last and the last first, many are called but few chosen. Indeed he did not hesitate to affirm that men will be judged, shown up as they really are, by the attitude they take to himself (cf. John 3. 17ff.).

There is always a judgement. But if this were all that John had to say, it is hard to understand how Jesus would or could have taken his work over. Was John's not also a message of salvation? In the Malachi passage, by which he was strongly influenced, it is said that before the great and terrible day Elijah would be sent to exercise a ministry of reconciliation – to turn the hearts of the fathers to the children and the hearts of the children to their fathers (Malachi 4. 5, 6). And this is certainly what was predicted, in the story of John's birth, to Zacharias – that he should make ready a people prepared for the Lord. Luke, moreover, adds from his own sources (Luke 3. 10ff.) that he offered the people a topical if rather limited programme of ethics, with nothing 'eschatological' about it, and presents him as a teacher of righteousness.

John told the crowds that there was One to come whose shoes he was not fit to take off: but he did not specify who it was. Later on, when he sent the messengers from prison (Matthew 11. 3; Luke 7. 20) he was not fully convinced that it was Jesus. ('He that should come' *need* not mean Messiah. It could mean no more than the prophet [?Elijah] who, according to some extra-biblical writings was to discover and then anoint Messiah.) The fourth Gospel, however, preserves another tradition, according to which Jesus had himself become for a time one of John's disciples and worked alongside of him, baptizing (John

3. 22, 23). This gave the Church the highest possible precedent for continuing to use water-baptism – baptizing converts 'into the name of Christ' – as a means to their receiving the Holy Spirit. (We may note that it was at Ephesus that St. Paul had found disciples [i.e. Christians] who 'knew only the baptism of John' and had not been introduced to the Christian rite.)

Now John declared that among his disciples ('one coming after me' means one of my followers) there was a man greater than himself, still to be recognized, who would supersede him. But in this source John, and not Jesus only, saw the descent of the Spirit at the Baptism and recognized the sign for which he was waiting. *Here* was the man anointed by the Spirit, for whom he had been sent to prepare the way; and to him he begins to transfer his own disciples (John **1.** 19–37; **3.** 22, 23).

This, then, was the witness of John who was sent to bear witness to the Light (John **1.** 7, 9), and that is his place in the Christian tradition.

* * *

As the people streamed down from Galilee to the Jordan valley in the South to be baptized, Jesus went too. It cannot have been on any sudden impulse, stimulated by popular excitement. He had far too independent a mind to be a 'joiner'; he was no conformist. We must not, like some of the popular 'lives' of Jesus, attribute imaginary motives to him. But if we ask why did he go? the answer must be bound up with another, what was he doing in all those years of waiting? Apart from one incident at the age of twelve (Luke **2.** 41–50) we do not know anything at all about him till he was a man of thirty. But all we know about human nature suggests that the words and deeds of his public ministry must have been laid down in thought and prayer and meditation during those 'silent years'. (There is nothing whatever to suggest that he went through any crisis of 'conversion'.) The loving observation of man and nature which was revealed in his teaching is evidence of how deeply he had reflected about life.

He had acquired a profound knowledge of the Scriptures,

which he was able to read in classical Hebrew, not out of the vernacular translation – and, apparently, to quote the Hebrew text in debate with learned ecclesiastics – and was putting his own interpretations on them. (If he had not been regarded as qualified, would he have been invited to 'read the Lesson' and afterwards to expound it or 'preach' [Luke **4.** 16ff.]? When the sermon came, it was more than they had bargained for; not the kind of sermon that churchwardens like, 'which could give no offence to anybody'.) He had trained himself to spend much time in prayer and he lived in constant awareness of the presence of God.

When the call came to him, he was not unprepared for it. There was that in his soul which responded to and accepted it. He must have been conscious of some great work awaiting him, and John's mission seemed to be the signal – a new call from God to his own people, to be the true 'remnant', to offer God true service; and with them he now identified himself and sought baptism at the hands of John.

But why did he go to a baptism of repentance? What had he to repent of? What need had he for remission of sins? (John's protest – Matthew **3.** 14 – reflects the perplexity in some early Christian circles about that.) What is meant by the reference in Christian language to his 'sinlessness'?

7

THE SINLESSNESS OF JESUS

IN traditional teaching and piety the meaning of the sinlessness of Jesus has been expounded far too negatively. The
mere absence of committed sin is not in itself any proof of
positive goodness, and it could consist with a weak and shallow
character that lacked the resolution to 'sin boldly'. Indeed,
when we speak about a 'blameless youth' we commonly mean
a young man who has not much in him. There is certainly no
sign in the Gospels that the Lord had any consciousness of sin.
Indeed everything shows the exact opposite. Nobody could
'convict him of sin' (John **8.** 46). A creative and cleansing
holiness went forth from him. All his life was a perfect self-
offering, in unbroken obedience to the will of God. This moral
and spiritual perfection is what Christians refer to as his
sinlessness.

But does that mean inability to sin (*non posse peccare*)? Does
it mean that he was, as it were, miraculously or supernaturally
protected against feeling the force of temptation or the possibility of wrong choices? For if so, he was not a real man, and
that conclusion has to be bluntly stated. Inability to make wrong
choices would mean that he was, in effect, a moral automaton
and the choices he did make would not be 'good' in any sense
that applies to human action, and his life would not have been
a moral achievement. Moreover, on that assumption, the Temp-
tation-story is describing no more than a staged episode. It
would not have been a real temptation at all, only a theological
make-believe in which he was just going through the motions.
And that is no less morally repugnant than it would be doctri-
nally disastrous. We must surely reject that interpretation of
sinlessness.

Or does it mean ability not to sin (*posse non peccare*)? Does it mean that he was so perfectly responsive to God, so receptive of his grace, that he was able to resist and conquer the temptations by which he was certainly assailed? That is a far more constructive approach to the question. He was not an automatic Saviour.

Young people have been heard to say that Jesus can offer them no moral example because he knew nothing of sexual temptation; but what possible ground is there for that suggestion? As I said above, if he was not tempted, then he did not fully share our human nature. But the writer of *Hebrews* just takes for granted that he was at all points tempted like as we are – only that he did not give way as we do (Hebrews **4.** 15). Like us, he grew, physically and morally (Luke **2.** 52, 40) and the Grace of God was upon him. He himself spoke of the disciples as 'continuing with me in my temptations' (Luke **22.** 28), and Luke observes that, after the Temptation, the devil departed from him, 'biding his time' (**4.** 13 *N.E.B.*). Jesus *learned* obedience by the things that he suffered. This was a real incarnation. He was in all things made like unto his brethren. All through his life, as in the Temptation story and in his encounter with the Demons, good is in conflict with evil. Jesus was the conqueror of evil, who was 'manifested to destroy the works of the devil'.[1]

The reference to Demons suggests a further important reflection. In the language of the Bible and Prayer Book, and in our own moral experience, Sin can mean and does mean two things. (1) It can mean 'our' sins, the sins that we commit by our own fault, our own grievous fault; or (2) the total complex of corporate evil, for which we are not directly responsible but into which all of us are born, by which all of us are limited and thwarted – it is harder for us to do right than wrong – by which ideal plans are too often wrecked, good motives conscripted into the service of evil, and history bedevilled and pulled off-course. Jesus 'knew how easily the soul of man could be crushed by the forces of evil organized into a system; and it was his challenge to such forces that brought him to his Cross'.[2]

[1] *Book of Common Prayer*, Collect for Epiphany 6.
[2] G. S. Duncan, *Jesus, Son of Man* (Nisbet, 1947), p. 39.

This is what St. Paul had in mind when he said that we wrestle not against flesh and blood but against . . . the world-rulers of this darkness (Ephesians **6.** 12, *R.V.*). This organized system of evil will (the Satanic Principalities and Powers) had been, he said, defeated and disarmed by Christ through his death and resurrection (Colossians **2.** 15).

This is what traditional Christian language commonly describes as original sin – original sin, not original guilt, for it is not our individual responsibility but the fatal legacy which we inherit. The idea was based on the story of the Fall, regarded as an actual event. We may regard the story of Paradise Lost not so much as giving the cause of our predicament as a myth intended to explain and emphasize it. Adam was not a historical personage. Adam means everyman – ourselves. But the facts remain. What original sin stands for is the moral solidarity of the race ('In Adam all die').

Now in *that* sense, Jesus certainly shared in sin. Though he was conceived by the Holy Spirit – however that phrase may be interpreted – he was nevertheless born of a human mother. The doctrine of the Immaculate Conception is an attempt to evade the implications of that by ascribing sinlessness to his mother. But – apart altogether from the objection that there is not the slightest scriptural warrant for it – that cuts at the root of the doctrine of Redemption. 'Jesus was born within the womb of a sinner, within the compass of our sinful flesh. As the Son of Adam he was born into our alienation, our God-forsakenness and darkness, and grew up within our bondage and ignorance, so that he had to beat his way forward by blows, growing, as Luke puts it, in wisdom and growing in grace before God as well as before man. He learned obedience by the things which he suffered; for that obedience within our humanity was a struggle with our sin and temptation.'[1] St. Paul speaks of him as being sent in the likeness of our sinful flesh that he might condemn sin in the flesh (Romans **8.** 3) – that is, in our sin-distorted human nature.

What we mean, therefore, by his sinlessness is that undefeated

[1] Torrance, op. cit., p. 132.

and inexhaustible goodness which triumphed over evil in all its forms, in the world around him and in his own life. And it is because he suffered, being tempted, that he is able to help those who are tempted (Hebrews 2. 18).

8

THE BAPTISM

I<small>N</small> the early Church the feast of the Epiphany was – and still
is in the Eastern Church today – the commemoration of the
Lord's Baptism – his conscious acceptance of his vocation
and, according to the fourth Gospel, the sign of his manifestation to Israel (John 1. 31–33). There are, as we have seen, two
traditions. What is fundamental to both of them is that in receiving baptism at John's hands Jesus passed through a profound spiritual experience, in which he 'saw' the Spirit
descending upon him and 'heard' a voice which declared
God's acceptance and gave him an inner assurance of his
mission.

Whether or not at this stage of his life he interpreted this in
terms of Messiahship is a question that invites learned mono-
graphs, but it matters little for the faith of Christians, and in
any case there can be no certain answer. There is no suggestion
in the Synoptics that he went about claiming to be Messiah –
all the evidence is the other way; and it is noticeable that in
the fourth Gospel John does not point to him as Messiah:
what he calls him is the Son of God and the Lamb that
takes away the sin of the world. (The reference is probably to Isaiah 53. 7.) What remains clear is that in this
experience, which opened the door to his public ministry,
there was given to Jesus the assurance, which was decisive
for everything that follows, that he stood in a special relationship to God, and was therefore charged with a unique
mission.

The content of the voice which he heard is concerned not
directly with Messiahship but with his relationship to God as
Father: thou art my Son, the beloved. This implies not just a
commission, as in the visions recorded of the prophets, or the

trust of a message to be delivered. What it implies, rather, is a *status*, a unique relationship to God.[1]

Later on, the Church had to attempt to formulate in terms of theology and metaphysics what that relationship ultimately implied, and the answer it gave is contained in the Nicene creed. That is beyond the scope of the present book. We must not read back into the mind of Jesus the dogmatic definitions of the fourth century. But in principle these theological developments have grown out of the Lord's own experience. The religion of which Jesus is the centre is inherent in the religion *of* Jesus, in his own personal religious faith. The consciousness of this filial relationship between himself and the God whom he knew as Father is the inner secret of his life, the source of his power, his authority and his Saviourhood.

The dove-symbol clothed in visual form the conviction which became no less determinative – that he was a man possessed by the Spirit of God. In the Old Testament, the Spirit of God 'comes upon' prophets and hero-figures to empower them for some particular task or enterprise. For Jesus this is a permanent reality (cf. John **1.** 33, *R.V.* – 'descending and *abiding* upon him'). Hence derives his message of deliverance (Luke **4.** 16ff.), hence the victory over the powers of evil. It was not merely that he was 'inspired' with a message, it was that God was operative through him. By the Spirit (or finger) of God he cast out devils. Of this he was totally convinced; and to say that he cast out devils by Beelzebub was for him the sin that has no forgiveness. It was blasphemy against the Holy Spirit. It was calling the Source of all goodness evil[2] (Mark **3.** 28–30. Matthew **12.** 24–32, Luke **12.** 10).

[1] See T. W. Manson, *The Teaching of Jesus* (C.U.P., 1931) pp. 101, 103.
[2] 'This is in truth the ultimate blasphemy, far beyond any profane taking of God's name in vain (or using the name of Jesus as a swearword), beyond intellectual atheism; for it is a flat denial of all spiritual values whatever. In the last resort it makes truth a delusion, conscience a disease, and reduces man's life to a tale told by a idiot . . . It is the worst and most deadly of all sins because it is the rejection of God's purpose and the denial of his nature; it is the betrayal of the cause of humanity – and it is spiritual suicide' – Manson, op. cit. p. 107, note 1.

It was through him that Christians received the Spirit, the Spirit that is creative of Christian character and that called into life the Christian society – the Community of the Holy Spirit. Whatever later theology may have to say, yet, taking the New Testament as a whole, 'The Spirit which we have received from God through Christ' and 'the Spirit of Christ' are interchangeable terms. (Notice 'the Spirit of Jesus' in Acts 16. 7, *R.V.*).

9

THE TEMPTATION

B UT after that great moment of intuition there came, as
there always does come, the reaction – the dark night of
the soul. (After any important decision we are nearly always assailed by doubts about it.) Could this really be true and
what did it mean? If he were truly and indeed the Anointed,
the Chosen Son of God, how would God work out his will
through him? How was he to interpret his divine office? There
followed the 'forty days' of the 'temptation' when he sought
the answer alone with God. (Forty days, in biblical usage, is a
conventional period of time [cf. 1 Kings **19.** 8; Acts **1.** 3]
but seems clearly meant here to recall the forty days of
Moses on the mountain and the forty years of Israel in the
desert.)

It was not just a time of quiet reflection, like the Buddha's
meditation under the Bo tree, but a tumultuous, harrowing experience. Mark's account uses violent language. The Spirit
drives him into the wilderness – the traditional abode of the
evil spirits – and he was there being tempted by Satan. The
narrative resounds with authenticity. That the Holy One was
tempted by the devil – the primitive Church would not have
invented *that*. Indeed it must have come, in the end, from himself – there is no other source from which it could have come –
though there may be some foreshortening of perspective, concentrating into a single incident the temptations and victories
of his lifetime. It is no good asking exactly what happened. No
onlooker would have seen anything, except perhaps the changing light in his eyes. The evangelists tell the story in haunting
imagery, but what happened was within his own soul.

Mark has, of course, no psychological interest. His concern
is not with the Lord's inward experience – he is not asking the

questions that we want to ask; his concern is to depict the
Messiah in this opening battle of his war on the demons and
the powers of evil. But he who conquered the devil in the world
without must encounter and defeat him in his own life. Whatever
it was, this was a *real* temptation, an assault on his integrity
and his will; and to say that implies that he might have failed.
For if the result were a foregone conclusion, if there were no
battle being fought out, then he was merely 'going through the
motions' – an idea which is morally repugnant – and it would
not have been a real temptation at all. But he won, and went
forward to his public mission with a victory already behind him.
Because he himself suffered, being tempted, he is able to help
those who are tempted (Hebrews **2.** 18).

We can rightly say that it was a moral triumph, but no
Christian will think that it was achieved without the operation
of God's grace in him, and the touch about the angels minister-
ing to him (in Mark, while the temptation was going on, not,
as in Matthew, after it was all over) may perhaps be a way of
saying just that.[1] 'Work out your own salvation . . . for it is
God who works in you' (Phil. **2.** 12, 13, *N.E.B.*) – that
apparent paradox of St. Paul's is something we know to be true
in Christian experience. May we not say that it was in the Lord's
too? (If we do say that, of course, we are approaching the question of his Person – who *is* he? – and of what the Church has
meant by the Incarnation.)

Unlike the first readers of the Gospels, what we want to know
is the content of the temptations, what it was that was going on
in the mind of Jesus. To ask that is perilous in the extreme, for
we cannot penetrate into his inner consciousness. Nor must we
make the mistake of attempting to read back modern ideas into
his mind, coloured as it was by his own time and place. Some
hints, however, are provided for us in the amplified version of
the story in Matthew **4.** 2–10; Luke **4.** 2–12 (presumably Q).
This appears to derive from a very different tradition, and it is

[1] Nineham suggests that the note about the wild beasts ('prowling
beasts about the way') may be, on the contrary, a reference to the idyll
of the messianic age in Isaiah **11.** 6–9.

so elaborately stylized that it looks as though it existed in written form as an early Christian sermon or 'instruction' long before the evangelists had access to it. Even so, the basic material must be due in its origin to the Lord himself, as later on he disclosed to the inner circle something of what he had been through in the wilderness. And both the actual context of the incident and the form in which it is here narrated seem to make clear that the content of the temptation was concerned with his understanding of his mission ('If thou art the Son of God . . .') and the siren voice suggesting short-cuts and some easier, less costly alternative. 'If you settle for second,' said President Kennedy, 'that is where you stay in life, I find.'

The story presupposes that he was conscious of being endowed with tremendous and unique powers, held under iron discipline and control. It is no temptation to me to possess myself of all the world's kingdoms and the glory of them. Who is this, who could have had it, and thrust it from him as a smaller thing than what he had come to do? Preachers and moralists warn us about our weaknesses. But, as tragic drama often exhibits, it can be a man's strength, his best gifts, that betray him – ambition may become demonic, love turn to blind jealousy and murder – if they are not submitted to the will of God. May we not say that all the three temptations described in the story come back, in the end, to one – to impose himself on the situation, treating his own will as though it were absolute, rather than seeking to learn and follow God's way, whatever the consequences to himself?

The form in which the narrative is presented may be said to relate the temptations pretty clearly to the popular expectations of the New Age and the role of Messiah as its inaugurator. There had always been the idea of the good time coming, a God-sent era of affluence and prosperity, when the ploughman should overtake the sower, the fig tree and the vine should yield their strength and men should eat in plenty and be satisfied. How bitter, by contrast, was the poverty prevalent, as he knew so well, in Palestine. (Nationalist sentiment went hand in hand with agrarian discontent about absentee landlords [cf. Mark **12.** 1–12 and parallels] and resentment of imperial taxation.)

Should he be the Messiah of a New Deal, righting the economic wrongs and turning stones, as it were, into bread? (Prolonged hunger generates food-fantasies and the smooth stones in a *wadi* may have suggested the round, flat loaves in common use.) There would have been spectacular support for that. He would have been giving the populace what they wanted and it *would* have been a beneficent revolution. But the heart of man's need would have been left untouched. Jesus knew what poverty meant (Luke **15.** 8, 9) and was deeply concerned with human physical need. He must clearly not be taken as disapproving such efforts as Oxfam and War-on-want or any attempts at social amelioration – they are indeed implicit in the Love-commandment. But, as our generation has learnt by experience, it does not follow that higher standards of life bring with them higher standards of living. He knew that man's deepest need is beyond the secular – an ultimate spiritual satisfaction (Matthew **5.** 3–10; **6.** 19–21, 25–33; cf. John **6.** 27). Man cannot live by bread alone.

Should he be the Davidic King-Messiah armed with temporal power and authority, setting them free from Roman occupation, establishing a golden-age theocracy and ruling over the world for its own good? There were centuries of scriptural hope behind that and it would have evoked an immediate response – indeed at the end the crowds turned against him when they realized that that was not what he meant. But absolute power tends to corrupt absolutely. Jesus was deeply distrustful of power (Mark **10.** 35–45); to usurp it meant to acknowledge the empire of Satan. In his kingdom the only strength is the strength of love; God alone is to be served and worshipped, and God's rule is not Napoleonic.

The third temptation (the second in Matthew's order) seems to turn on current apocalyptic visions of Messiah riding on the clouds – a more than earthly, supernatural figure who with the breath of his lips should slay the wicked (cf. 2 Thessalonians **2.** 8) and establish a new heaven and a new earth. Why not dazzle the people into accepting him by some sheer display of magical, pseudo-miraculous, pseudo-religious exhibition? The Church has succumbed to that many a time. But that was what he steadfastly refused to do. Jesus would coerce no man's judgement and would force no man's allegiance. That way he now once and for all rejected.

But we can, perhaps, find a deeper meaning here. This was the temptation to force the hand of God. Throw yourself down from the pinnacle of the Temple (as we might say, the dome of St. Paul's) and put God's providence to the test. No harm will happen to you. The Psalmist says that the angels in their hands shall bear thee up. What that amounted to was the demand for that kind of 'supernatural' intervention which would abrogate in his favour the laws by which God's world is ordered – the guarantee that God would protect his Son against the contingencies of man's life on earth, so that he could be kept safe and avoid the cost – to be a 'saved' Messiah, not a Saviour. 'Thou shalt not tempt the Lord thy God.' The temptation came back and struck him between the eyes in Peter's protest at Caesarea Philippi (Mark **8.** 32), and hence the vehement 'Behind me – *Satan!*'

When St. Paul spoke of the Son 'born under the law' (Galatians **4.** 4) he was saying more than he knew. The Messiah, the Revealer, is at all points subject to the conditions of our humanity. He is not exempt from the laws under which man lives – it is not in that sense that he was the Mediator of a 'supernatural' and eternal life. God sends his rain on the just and on the unjust – so generous is he. But God has no 'favourites'. Things are what they are and life must be accepted as 'given', with all its apparent callousness and cruelty – and that points to the truth that this world is a vale of soul-making. On his last night on earth, in Gethsemane, Jesus had finally to face the knowledge that there would be no 'legions of angels'. God's love would not intervene even to save the only-begotten Son. The cup that was given to him he must drink. But when he said 'Thy will be done', that was not a whimper of resignation but the creative acceptance of the situation as it was, seeing the tragedy as the means to moral and spiritual victory, both for himself and for all mankind.

People ask 'Why has this happened to me? I prayed to be saved from it. Does God not care? Did I not pray hard enough?' Jesus prayed in an agony of bloody sweat. Some in their sufferings turn against God and hate him. Jesus trusted God to the end, and a few hours later with his dying breath commended his spirit into the Father's hands. And it was because of this St. Paul could say that neither life nor death nor the powers of evil nor present nor future can separate us from the love of God which is in Christ Jesus our Lord.

Bribery, force and magic the Lord rejected, though the Church has not always been so faithful. He would take upon himself the form of the Servant, identified with all human need and suffering, and in and through that reveal the reign of God – the Kingdom and the Power and the Glory. Whether or not he yet fully realized in the wilderness all that was implied in it, the decision he made carried him to Calvary. He learned obedience by the things that he suffered.

10

PROCLAIMING THE GOOD NEWS

IT appears that after John was arrested Jesus believed that his
own hour had come. He moved down from the hill-town of
Nazareth to the village of Capernaum by the Lakeside and
stepped forward into his public ministry. But his message was
not the same as John's. John had prepared, Jesus brought the
answer. It begins with the proclamation of good news. 'The
time is fulfilled and the Kingdom of God has come near. Repent and believe the good news' (Mark **1**. 14, 15). All these
words need careful examination.

The time is fulfilled – time meaning, here, God's time. We
think of time as a rectilinear movement, a stream in which we
are all being swept along, unending and ever-changing process;
and it seems to have in itself no meaning. The Greeks found
meaning only in the unchanging, in the eternal reality of being,
of which the empirical world of change and becoming was at
best an imperfect image or reflection. For Greek thought the
temporal is but half-real – that is why it had no philosophy of
history and found it hard to take with full seriousness the real
human nature of the Son of God; whatever reality 'becoming'
had, it derived from its participation in or reflection of the unchanging Forms of Being. As Plato put it, God had made time
to be a moving image of eternity.

This idea of a two-level universe, in which the whole pano-
rama of events reflects, points to and finds its meaning in a
higher, invisible and eternal order, has dominated Western
philosophy and the traditional pattern of theology. On the
whole, contemporary thought rejects it. Philosophy has de-
bunked metaphysics, and the Platonic tradition in theology is
now widely assumed to be finally out of court. We tend to think
that becoming, the time-process, is the only reality there is. For

us too, therefore, it is difficult to find any transcendent meaning in successive events or in life itself.

But the Bible looks at time in a different way. The whole Bible rests on the conviction that historical events in time are the sphere of God's operation and the medium of his self-disclosure; in them 'the arm of the Lord' is revealed. Therefore they have a qualitative meaning. They cannot be measured simply by pointer-readings. History is more than a mere chronicle – it involves interpretation. The Greek Bible uses the idea of Time in the sense of occasion, or, as we might say, *timing*. Things happen when God, so to speak, is ready for them. When the fullness of time had come the Christ was born (Galatians **4.** 4). Fulfilment is one of the Christian root-ideas.

The burden of early Apostolic preaching was that what had long been preparing in the faith and experience of Israel, God had now fulfilled in Jesus Christ (Acts **3.** 18). The Fathers had lived in an age of expectation, now the age of fulfilment had come. The past is past and all things are now being made new (2 Corinthians **5.** 17). That is what Jesus had said about his own mission. The time is fulfilled, God is now ready. All through the long years of history the seed has been secretly growing and maturing, God's purposes have been ripening fast (steadfastly); now the corn is up and the harvest waiting (Mark **4.** 10ff.). This is the time, the occasion, of fulfilment. We are not waiting for God to do something. God is doing something. He is at work now. As he said in the first sermon at Nazareth, 'Today is this Scripture fulfilled in your ears!'

I think we can hardly exaggerate the excitement with which Jesus received and made public that intuition. We have so far formalized the Gospel and so far conventionalized him, that it does not now sound like an intoxicating and revolutionary proclamation, a message to turn the world upside down. He believed that he and his contemporaries were involved in one of the crises of history, indeed the supreme crisis of history, in which life and death decisions would have to be made, and the stake was nothing less than the soul of man. 'What shall a man give in exchange for his soul?' Opportunity rejected means judgement, and he gave tremendous warnings about that. But what he was offering was opportunity, unbelievable unimagined opportunity, which he wanted to have shouted from the house-tops (Matthew **10**. 27; Luke **12**. 3). Forget the old ideas and believe the good news!

'Repent' means far more than repenting our sins. It means a radical change of heart and mind, seeing life in a different frame of reference, looking out at the world from a changed centre, a total redirection of thought and experience. We commonly say that idealistic schemes will fail because 'you can't change human nature'. Jesus *starts* by demanding just that, being born again, becoming as little children. Only so can we enter the Kingdom of God.

That must not be taken to mean that there is required of us a conventional experience of 'conversion'. Many Christians have never been through that at all, and Jesus himself was not of the 'twice-born' type. Nor does it mean that we have to be 'mystics' before we can understand the good news. He dealt with that in two well-known parables – the Hidden Treasure and the Pearl of Great Price.

These describe two very different kinds of men. The first was a peasant or smallholder – and nothing could be less 'mystical' than a peasant, hard as nails, with mainly material values, who, finding a cache of treasure in his holding and realizing that it could introduce him to an entirely different kind of life, makes up his mind that at all costs he must have it. He decides to sell up and buy the field. The pearl-merchant was a connoisseur, a man whose professional training and experience had taught him appreciation of fine things and discrimination of aesthetic values. Where could he find absolute satisfaction? When he came across the pearl that set the value of all other pearls, he recognized what all his life he had been looking for. He decided to make the plunge and buy it. These were men of very different temperament who came to their heart's desire along different roads, but from both alike it required the total price. The Kingdom of God, said Jesus, is 'like' that.

It need not involve a crisis of conversion, though for some it does, and perhaps must, involve that. But for everyone it involves being 'born again'. We shall never be able to enter into the creative originality of his mind if we measure him by our presuppositions instead of learning to measure ours by his. What he had to tell the world was not merely something about a revised form of piety, but about a new way of experiencing life. He is not imposing on it an abstract formula, he is reading life and telling us what he finds in it and showing us what he finds through his response to it. And the central category of his experience, the leading motive of all his teaching, was what he began to proclaim – the Kingdom of God.

This was not a phrase which he had himself coined, but one into which he read deeper meanings; and no words, not even his own, can exhaust them. The phrase stands for the creative vision in which he lived and moved and had his being, not merely an article in a creed or a topic for theological discussion.[1] He is not just trying, as many preachers do, to reanimate and invite re-acceptance of a theological phrase that had gone dead. He is telling us what he lived by. What that was cannot be verbally expounded, it can only be recognized in his living. But he had to use words for its communication, and he is using the only words available to communicate his mind to an audience brought up, like himself, in the Jewish tradition.

The phrase in itself was a theological commonplace. Indeed, the idea of God's rule or sovereignty – for it means that, not an area or territory, like the kingdom of Great Britain and Northern Ireland – runs through and dominates the Old Testament. When we today speak about the Kingdom we are probably thinking in sociological terms, of some idealized order of society which, as we hope, will one day be realized as the end or goal of historical evolution – the one far-off divine event to which the whole creation moves. But neither for the Old Testament nor for him was that the primary meaning of the phrase. It means God's kingly rule accepted. That, of course, implies social righteousness, as all the great prophets had insisted; but it is God-centred, not man-centred.

[1] See Manson, op. cit. p. 161.

We shall never get anywhere near the mind of Jesus if we do not first understand that God is for him the central and absolute Reality – which for modern men is so hard to understand. The major premise of all his ethical teaching, as someone has said, is the Kingdom of God. For him, therefore, the Kingdom is not something to be built by human enterprise and idealism in England's green and pleasant land; it is of God's gift and under God's initiative: 'it is your Father's good pleasure to give you the kingdom' (Luke 12. 32). Nor is it a state of affairs that will prevail at some remote and not too probable future – as we commonly say, 'at Kingdom Come'. It is 'the great existing reality'. What he proclaimed was that it had arrived.[1]

It is, for him, the real Presence of God.

For the current religious thought of his time, however, it seemed that the realization of God's rule or sovereignty was delayed and thwarted, for it was opposed by the pseudo-kingdom of Satan. It could, therefore, only be realized on earth when the rival empire was overthrown; and in the popular writings of the time this was taken to mean that there first must be and would be a spectacular supernatural intervention, when God would break into the course of history to annihilate the usurping powers of evil – not excluding the oppressors of Israel – and establish his reign in a new and purified world-order. This, with manifold variations, was the theme of the 'apocalyptic' books through which the teaching of the prophets now found its way into popular religion. This, of course, coloured the

[1] This is the thesis of Dodd's magisterial books. He urges that the Aramaic behind 'has come near' in Mark 1. 15 ought rather to be translated 'is here now', and that this is the theme of all the parables. ('Realized eschatology.') That translation is not undisputed. But Jesus certainly speaks of 'receiving' and 'entering into' the Kingdom, and he said it is 'within you' (almost certainly that [and not 'among you'] Luke 17. 21). He taught us to pray 'Thy kingdom come', and the meaning of that is 'Thy will be done'; and told stories about the mustard-seed and the leaven, indicating the growth and development of the Kingdom. But that is the fuller realization of a reality already present. The Kingdom 'comes' as God's rule is acknowledged. The probable meaning of the perfect tense in Mark 9. 1 is 'till they see or recognize the Kingdom as something having already come'.

minds of the Lord's hearers, and it must be probable that at various points it has coloured the tradition of his own sayings – how deeply can only be discerned by close examination of each one.

What he said about the Kingdom sets him apart from the other religious leaders of his day. 'They anticipated a coming kingdom; Jesus declared that the time for its coming was now. They discussed the time and the manner of its coming; Jesus laid down the conditions on which men could "enter" it. They taught that it would come by divine *fiat*, as if God were meanwhile withholding it; Jesus taught that it was God's good pleasure to give it now, if only men would "receive" it. Their hopes were fed on apocalyptic dreams; Jesus 'took his stand securely on ethical and spiritual principles.'[1] There is nothing apocalyptic in the first sermon. It proclaims the presence of God in power and healing; and it proclaims implicitly that where Jesus is, there the Kingdom of God has come near (cf. Matthew **13**. 16–18; Luke **10**. 23, M Q).

This was the inner certainty of his whole mission – that the world is maintained by a holy and loving will, that people matter because God loves and cares for them and that this is the final meaning of our existence. To live in communion with Reality is to enter into life – real life, or, as St. John puts it, eternal life. This is life eternal, to know the only true God and Jesus Christ whom he has sent (John **17**. 3). There is thus an essentially other worldly reference in his own life and in all his teaching. Yet he certainly would not have admitted the distinction between 'sacred' and 'secular'. Where God is king all life is hallowed. If he was asked what the Kingdom of God is 'like', his images and pictures were drawn from ordinary weekday experience, in the kitchen, the field, the vineyard and the fishing-smack. It *is* 'in heaven', it is 'to come' on earth.

This tension, this bi-polarity, is integral to the Christian response to life, which is neither 'religionless' nor pietistic, which can never be completely at home in this world yet never regards religion as an escape from it. Perhaps it could rightly be said

[1] Duncan, op. cit. pp. 46, 47.

that in the long run the Kingdom of God is the realm of right relations. For when men are in the right relationship to God, who is the reality of all that is real, they will be rightly related to the world, to their fellows and to themselves. It involves the transformation of all experience.

* * *

That sense of God's nearness and immediacy which pervades the whole ministry of Jesus, is the lifegiving spiritual atmosphere in which the first believers had their being and from which they drew their joy and spontaneity; and it was from the Lord himself that they derived it. If for most of us now God seems remote – or, as many people say, 'unreal' – we shall get no help and indeed may be gravely injured by trying to stimulate in ourselves emotions which are not sincerely and genuinely felt. For that is merely religious sentimentalism. Religious 'feeling' is of no great importance and is largely a matter of psychological make-up. Nor need we worry too much about the word 'God', spoilt, as it tends to be now, by unhappy overtones. If we want again to experience the reality, which is more important than any names we use, we must put ourselves to school with the Master of living, to learn what he has to show us about life and the supernatural quality at the heart of it.

Meanwhile, he said, mankind must choose, between reality and illusion, creativity and destruction, life and death. 'The absolute Sovereignty of God,' says Manson, 'is not a dogma accepted on the authority of a tradition, nor the conclusion of a philosophical inquiry; it is a postulate of religious faith.'[1] It has to be proved true in a man's own soul. 'Thy kingdom come' means 'Thy will be done' – and done, primarily, in myself. So men must make decisions and take sides. They must face the king when he takes account of his servants. Would they gain the whole world and lose their own souls? No other decision is comparable in urgency. A great part of his recorded teaching was concerned with uncovering that crisis, setting forth the imperative claims and obligations of God's kingdom present in

[1] Manson, op, cit. p. 167.

the world, pointing them to the gate that leads into life, and summoning them to what, in the current jargon, would be called an existential decision. We shall look at the teaching more closely in a later section.

* * *

The Kingdom of God must not be sentimentalized, or equated with private ideals of our own, or the best elements in civilization. For Jesus it meant something *decisive* – the Word and Act of God at the last time. God's time is fulfilled and the Kingdom is here. He claimed 'that the last time had come with him and around him, and that he was authorized by God to preach the Gospel of the last time . . . Plainly Jesus did in some form proclaim that with him the *eschaton* (end), the last act, had come . . . The proclamation of the Kingdom of God as the End, the last Act of God, is a focus that brings together coherently more of the teachings ascribed to Jesus than any other. It is quite consonant with the intellectual and religious atmosphere of first-century Judaism, and it accounts for the Church's eschatological interpretation of Jesus, which would otherwise be largely inexplicable.[1] No doubt there are many other sides to the teaching of Jesus. No doubt there are many individual characteristic elements in it which we cannot and should not too glibly account for by ascribing them to contemporary influences and sources. But that this teaching was given within a framework of eschatological urgency, as a message from God of final importance, because delivered in the final Age, we cannot doubt'.[2]

[1] e.g. the persistent New Testament language about the Coming of Christ and the End.
[2] C. P. R. Hanson, in *Difficulties for Christian Belief* (Macmillan, 1967), p. 49.

F

11

THE MINISTRY OF THE KINGDOM

THE Ministry starts with the calling of disciples. Mark describes the call of four leading figures in the early history of Christianity, and naturally puts Peter first. (In Luke, Peter is called at a later stage [Luke **5.** 1–11].) Others were to join them; not the Twelve only, but apparently a large number of men and women – we hear of 'the multitude of his disciples' – who moved about with him from place to place. About most of them we know virtually nothing; even the list of the Twelve is not quite certain.

We do not know what it was that he sought or found in those whom he would train for discipleship. What was it, we ask, that he had seen in Judas? Jesus was limited in his human knowledge, but with his incomparable moral insight he was surely never mistaken about character? They were certainly not infallible nor sin-proof; again and again they were to disappoint him.

But what he cared for most was the single eye – integrity and purity of heart. What he approved was the decisive character which keeps its eye on the furrow and does not look back, which knows what it wants and knocks on the door to ask for it (Matthew **7.** 7) and is prepared to pay the price it costs. The fishermen whom he called from the lakeside were men who were ready to keep nothing back, to burn their boats behind them and commit themselves. He would not accept disciples on easier terms (Mark **8.** 34; Matthew **7.** 14; Luke **9.** 57–8). The disciple, said Jesus, must count the cost or he may find too late that he cannot face it (Luke **14.** 28ff.). What the full price would be they had yet to learn. Could they drink the cup that he would have to drink?

It does not follow, of course, that all Christians are called to

abandon their homes and their work – that would bring human
society to an end – any more than the imitation of Christ means
living exactly in the way that he lived. Those were the terms of
a special vocation. In every generation there will be Christians
needed for and called to special vocations of religious witness
or ministries of succour which may entail poverty and celibacy.
The Christian vocation of the great majority, and it may in fact
be harder rather than easier, will be to serve God and follow
Christ in their families and the earning of their livelihood. The
outward conditions of life will be very different, but from all is
required the same consecration; and this is what is meant by
'secular sanctity'.

The Rabbis all gathered disciples round them, as Saul sat at
the feet of Gamaliel. But these were pupils in the scholastic
sense, or as lawyers would now put it, in chambers. The disciples of Jesus had to learn more than could be found in text-
books. For them discipleship meant initiation. To be a disciple
in the school of Jesus – 'taking the yoke' of Jesus on them (Matthew 11. 29) – meant education into his way of life, and, as he
warned them, learning how to suffer. St. Paul speaks about
'learning Christ as the truth is in Jesus' (Ephesians 4. 20 – cf.
Acts 9. 16; Philippians 3. 10) and it takes more than threescore
years and ten. Christians are 'learning' to the end. We are still
unfinished disciples when we die. Can a Christian believe that
his education stops and marks are finally made up at half-term?

The Gospel narratives are not entirely clear, but what seems
to emerge from them is that there were two concentric circles.
The disciples, the larger body, were the candidates from whom
he selected the inner circle of intimates, the Twelve whom he
was to name 'Apostles' (Luke 6. 13).[1] They were sent out as
heralds of the Kingdom, but their first and primary function
was 'to be with him' (Mark 3. 14) and much of the later part of
the Ministry was devoted to their intensive training. These were
the men, the 'earthen vessels', to whom he was to entrust his
cause in the world. On these twelve limited, ordinary men, there

[1] The chief references are Mark 3. 13–19; 6. 7–13; Matthew 10; Luke
6. 13–17 and 9. 1–6.

was, under the providence of God, to depend the rise and extension of Christianity.

There is much debate whether the Lord intended to found an institutional church. Matthew clearly implies that he did – a view which 'liberal' scholarship tends to repudiate. But undoubtedly he did found the Church, the society created by his Spirit; and the germ was already present in the Twelve and those 'who companied with us all the time that the Lord Jesus went in and out among us' (Acts 1. 21). That pre-resurrection community was disrupted. When the shepherd was smitten the sheep were scattered (Mark 14. 27; Zechariah 13. 7). All the disciples forsook him and fled. When he was restored to them by forgiveness – and the Christian Church was founded in forgiveness – they became the nucleus of the new fellowship (*Koinonia*). Their association with the Lord, their having been specially trained and taught by him, and their having been witnesses of the Resurrection, gave them place of unquestioned authority. To be 'in Christ' was to be in the *Koinonia*; and that meant to continue 'steadfastly in the Apostles' teaching and fellowship' (Acts 2. 42).

The etymological meaning of the name 'Apostle' is 'one who is sent, a missionary'. 'As the Father has sent me, even so send I you' (John 20. 21). Indeed the word is used in the New Testament in that wider sense and not only of the Twelve. The Church is the apostolic Church, not only in the meaning of being built on the foundation of the Apostles and prophets, Jesus Christ himself being the head corner-stone (Ephesians 2. 20, cf. Revelations 21. 14), but also in the meaning of being a *sent* Church, charged with a missionary, apostolic ministry. The whole aim of the Pharisaic system was to gather a saved minority out of the world, protected behind the fence of the law. He would send a saving minority into the world.[1]

'As he passed by' he saw men and summoned them, making

---

[1] When St. Paul accused Peter of withdrawing, or separating, himself from the Gentiles at Antioch (Galatians 2. 11, 12) he may have meant 'behaving like a Pharisee (as I did myself before my conversion)' (see Manson, op. cit. pp. 240–43).

an unqualified demand, which was given spontaneously and without question. What a light that throws on the 'authority', the uniqueness of moral and spiritual stature which disclosed itself to his followers! While he lived with them as man among men, completely identified with their common life, they discerned in him something more, something that transcends human experience, something 'supernatural', which *claims* people and calls them in question. 'Just a man', 'One of ourselves' – but is that all? Will that account for what actually happened? No interpretation of Jesus can be true which cannot account for the rise of Christianity!

Modern anti-Christian propagandists are laying down very strange conditions when they insist that the only people whose opinions about him are bound to be untrustworthy are Christians – that is, those who know most about him – whereas those who are anxious to discredit him can be better trusted to form 'objective' judgements.

Mark's breathless narrative hurries the reader out into the open arena of human need – the crowds with their ephemeral excitements, the beggars, the blind, the cripples, the lunatics, the whole vivid, noisy, oriental scene, the crowds made up, as we know, with their burdens of suffering and guilt. Jesus steps into it as the Healer. This work became more and more exacting, apparently draining his spiritual vitality (Mark 5. 30) – he could only stand it by night-long vigils of prayer (1. 35) – leaving him no time for meals or sleep (3. 20; 5. 24), no privacy.

Yet he felt constrained to move from one place to another, everywhere thronged by people making demands on him, never refusing any cry for help. He ignored the crowds to pick out the individual. People mattered to him more than 'movements'. Where human need was, there he must be. That was the vocation of the Son of Man. And this was the good news of God in action. This was how he began the Ministry of the Kingdom.

12

THE MIRACLES

HERE at once we encounter the question of Miracles. If we try to cut the miracles out of the story there will hardly be any story left, and what is left will not be Christianity. We cannot 'commend it to modern men' that way, for we should in fact be commending something else. There is no non-miraculous Christianity.

But the whole debate and controversy about miracles has for far too long been conducted on the wrong ground, concentrating on oddness or abnormality or alleged violations of the laws of nature, as if those were the most important things about them; and Christians have appealed to these interventions into the normal sequences of nature as evidence that God was at work in them, or as 'proofs' of the divinity of Jesus.

But the Christian case, if put forward on those grounds, will be lost: and more than that, it ought to be lost. It is, in effect, an appeal to the God in the gaps. But that is an eighteenth-century war, not our war. That battlefield was really abandoned long ago. It is not there that the Bible confronts the modern man. The Bible is not asking our questions. It knows nothing of secondary causes, but sees everything that happens in nature, or in history, as the direct act of God. But whatever happens by the act of God, or by the initiative of the human will, happens within and through the processes of secondary 'natural' causation. If mental illness is cured by physical treament, or pneumonia by antibiotics, the cure is no less the act of God for that, even though it will not make the headlines or be popularly described as miraculous.

Thus the real question begins much further back. The difficulty about the Gospel miracles is, as Dodd remarks, a comparatively minor one. The major question is whether the whole Bible from beginning to end rests on a mistake – whether the world is more than a closed system determined by its own internal causation, or whether it is ultimately dependent on a transcendent Purpose which sustains it. This is belief in God as the Bible and Christianity understand it. The Bible is not concerned, it must be remembered, to produce arguments for God's existence. It is the book of a worshipping community, and belief in God is its presupposition. A worshipping community does not ask whether the God it worships is real. A God who may or may not exist, and about whose existence argument is necessary, is not what any religion means by God.

Now what makes a miracle miraculous, in any sense that matters to religion, is not its oddness or its abnormality or its interruption of the 'laws' of nature – observed and predicted regularities; it is its character as revelation, an event through which God is disclosed to faith. The miracles of healing are less abnormal, less deviations from ordinary experience, than some of the others, like walking on the water. Most people today are prepared to accept the healings, as being supported by clinical experience, whereas the others are just 'things that don't happen'. But the former are, in the real sense, much *more* miraculous. They reveal to us something far more important, and at greater depth, about God, and his will and purpose for mankind. And that is how the New Testament understands them; 'mighty works' the synoptic Gospels call them; not portents, but signs and disclosures of the Spirit of God. And it was so that Jesus himself regarded them.

> *The Spirit of the Lord is upon me because he anointed*
> *   me to preach good tidings to the poor,*
> *He hath sent me to proclaim release to the captives*
> *   and recovering of sight to the blind,*
> *To set at liberty them that are bruised*
> *   to proclaim the acceptable year of the Lord...*

'Today is this scripture fulfilled in your ears' (Luke 4. 18, 19, 21b)

What the prophets had hoped for, God was now doing. These were signs that the Kingdom had arrived.[1]

But here we must empty our minds of a fatal and too long unchallenged misconception which befogs the whole story with unreality – that Jesus went about claiming to be God and was performing his miracles to 'prove' it. Jesus never said that he was God. Nor was he concerned to vindicate his claims. It is true, no doubt, that all through the centuries Christians have appealed to the miracles as 'evidence', and sometimes the Gospels appeal to them in that way. But the Lord himself was not interested in 'evidences'. Only the insecure are self-conscious. He was far too sure of God and of his mission, and so of himself, to be on the defensive. His actions were entirely spontaneous. If he had wanted to use the cures as 'proofs' would he have said 'Tell no man'? He was not healing people to 'prove' anything. Still less was he doing it in the expectation that they might be persuaded to 'go to church' in consequence. His eye was far too single for that. He was helping people because they needed help. It angered him that people should have to suffer so.[2] That was not what God wills for his children.

There is no support in his attitude for the notion that suffering or illness are 'sent', for our good or as punishment for sin – Christians are prone to talk far too glibly about the 'purifying effect of suffering' (cf. John 9. 3). (Illness, of course, may be a result of sinful conduct and often is – e.g. syphilis; but this is not at all the same thing.) These things were, for him, invaders in his Father's world, and wherever he met them he 'cast them out'. When the pitiful leper came into his presence, thereby breaking all the regulations, Jesus stretched out his hand and *touched* him – and if anything is a miracle it is that. There was a disclosure of God, if anywhere. This is how God deals with men.

[1] I attempted some discussion of miracles in general terms in my first course given under this Trust, and will not repeat here what I tried to say then. See *Questioning Faith* (ch. 6). Also, more importantly, Alan Richardson, *The Miracle stories of the Gospels* (S.C.M., 1941).

[2] At Mark 1. 41 the 'western' text reads 'moved with anger' for 'moved with compassion', and because of its obvious difficulty is probably the right reading.

God does not wait until we are clean. 'While we were yet sinners Christ died for us' (Romans 5. 8). To a man haunted by some burden of guilt which had induced a functional paralysis Jesus gave the gift of forgiveness, so that he arose and took up his bed and walked (Mark 2. 1–12). He was as sight to the blind and feet to the lame.

It hurt him to think that ecclesiastical rules should stand between men and release from their infirmities. If, he said, the Sabbath is the Lord's day, how ought the Lord's day to be observed? Is it right to save a life or to kill? (Mark 3. 1–6; Luke 13. 10–16). On that he would have no evasion or subterfuge, and he cured the man with a calculated publicity. Whether or not at the time he was fully aware of it, he was writing the first sentence of his own death-warrant. This was what began the official opposition. 'The Sabbath was made for man, not man for the Sabbath.'

That phrase, which has never been forgotten, can be and not infrequently is, misused to defend a mere impatience of discipline and to justify the neglect of religious duty. But it announced a religious revolution. It was an open repeal or abrogation not only of the Pharisaic system but also of much that is found in the Old Testament. It applies to far more than the Sabbath in particular, and Churchmen still need to be reminded of it. In the sight of God, as Jesus understood him, human need always takes precedence over any ecclesiastical regulations.

Contemporary Jewish belief – which had been very considerably influenced during the Exile by the Iranian cult now commonly called Zoroastrianism – was that, while God's sovereignty was absolute yet it was for the time thwarted and opposed by the rival empire of the powers of evil which was plotting to bring the human race to ruin. Disease, due to possession by the demons – a view which was shared, ostensibly, by Jesus – was one instance of their dark dominion. Accordingly, in casting out devils he was engaged in the great cosmic conflict which is being fought out in the soul of every man, between light and darkness, life and death. ('We wrestle not against flesh and blood but against . . . the world-rulers of this darkness' – Ephesians **6.** 12). He was indeed breaking down the barriers between man and that plenitude of life which is God's will for him, and his gift to those in whose hearts the Kingdom of God is central. He was offering men wholeness, salvation.

Some of those barriers they had themselves erected by their own false ideas about God, thinking of him as one who was hostile to sinners. His much-criticized friendship with sinners, his constant concern with bringing home the lost sheep – his gesture, for example, to Zacchaeus (Luke **19.** 1–10) so that this despised and unlovable little man stood up 'saved' in all his human dignity – all this was part of his throwing down of barriers and his ministry of reconciliation. He was reconciling men to God by revealing to them God's care for men.

The whole Ministry, not his death alone, should thus be interpreted as an at-one-ment; and theology will run into a cul-de-sac if it tries to interpret the Atonement exclusively in terms of his death. Jesus was more than a 'portrait' or 'image' of God. Classical Christian faith has always affirmed that in him and through him God was *doing* something, which has changed the whole human situation. The works of healing were one manifestation of it.

As this healing ministry developed, in the early days, Jesus was aware that the power of God was present and at work in it – that it was a sign that the Kingdom was winning. (It was in that sense, but only in that sense, that he regarded the miracles as 'evidence'.) This comes out in his message to John the Baptist – 'Go and tell John what you see and hear' (Matthew **11.** 4ff., Luke **7.** 22ff.). (Was John still genuinely convinced, or was he trying to force the hand of Jesus? He seems to have wanted what many people today demand of the Church, something more spectacular, a revolution rather than a ministry.) It comes out again in his exultant answer when the Seventy reported their exorcisms: 'I beheld Satan as lightning fall from heaven' (Luke **10.** 17, 18 – cf. Isaiah **14.** 12). The giant in armour had met his conqueror (Mark **3.** 27).

*　　*　　*

Belief in Christ and in Christianity does not depend on accepting that every miracle happened exactly as it is recorded – or even that it happened at all.[1] But the total impression left by the stories reflects a real historical situation. In him and through him there was operative a moral and spiritual 'dynamic', an invincible energy of goodness, overcoming the resistance of evil and the barriers of despair, guilt and fear. The outward-moving holiness of his being brought healing and newness of life to all who were touched by it. It was not the holiness of separation, it was the holiness of the love that saves.

[1] The finding of the coin in the fish's mouth, mentioned only in Matthew's special source (Matthew 17. 24–27) is rightly regarded with great suspicion. A stock story in classical folk-lore it is told, in a different form, by Herodotus. But, in fact, it is not even said that it did happen!

13

JESUS AS TEACHER

'WHAT is this?' said the crowd. 'A new . . . teaching!' (Mark **1.** 27, *N.E.B.*); and it *was* radical and revolutionary. Yet 'the strength of the Gospel does not lie in the revelation of new and unexpected truths, but rather in its proclamation that the deepest hopes and yearnings of men may now find fulfilment.'[1] This was because the Kingdom of God had arrived – the keynote of the whole proclamation.

Jesus spent a great deal of his time in teaching, and, as we have seen, the Q document is mainly a record of characteristic sayings. Through them his thought echoes down the centuries. The profound impression made by the Lord's teaching is reflected in many phrases in the Gospels. 'The people all hung upon him, listening' (Luke **19.** 48). Not all crowds, or classes, behave like that! Others reacted violently against it and 'sought counsel to put him to death'. What was certain was that nobody could ignore it. But as popular piety has done what might have been supposed to be impossible and made him unexciting and uninteresting – a lay-figure rather than a Person – so it has conventionalized his teaching, allegorizing and 'spiritualizing' it, or, using it as though it were a textbook of formalized theological propositions, to such an extent as largely to disguise its creative originality and force.

I cannot here attempt any proper study or even a summary of what he taught. That requires a whole book to itself; and almost every section of this book uses material drawn from his own words. I can only attempt to give some description of the Teacher at work and his teaching methods, and to suggest the right way of approach if we are to take to ourselves what he taught.

[1] Duncan, op. cit. p. 278.

Jesus was an incomparable teacher – the Master of all who teach. Untrained in the modern discipline of 'pedagogic psychology', he had a supreme understanding of human nature. He knew and studied the Bible in depth, and we go badly wrong if we underrate the massive intellectual strength and the vital thought which underlies the teaching; but there is no evidence of other reading. What he taught was not 'got up' out of books. It came direct from his own experience – his knowledge of God and his observation of life. That was its 'authority' – 'I say unto you'.

It must be remembered that he was oriental, and thought in pictures rather than in abstractions; he was not expounding texts like a theologian so much as presenting images like a poet. And not only had he a poet's imagination; much of what he said can rightly be called poetry. It is possible, even after two translations, to arrange whole sections of his recorded sayings in the rhythms and structures of Hebrew 'Parallelism'.[1] The imaginative quality of his thinking and his wonderful artistry in the use of words shine out most brilliantly in the parables – surely the best story-telling in all literature. He also had a keen sense of the ridiculous – we are so afraid of letting him be human that it has seemed impious to recall that – and some of his sayings must have been greeted with laughter. He had a complete mastery of his subject-matter and a marvellous 'empathy' in communicating it. Here are all the natural endowments of a great teacher and a great artist – for what he taught was not only true religion, it was also a superb work of art.

Great themes rather than mere techniques are the first secret of greatness in speech or writing. Strong thought clothes itself in strong phrases, and the 'right' phrases for what it wants to say; weak thought in flaccid or self-conscious language. The great speaker or writer is able, or has learnt, to make words say what he really means. Jesus never used tired clichés or the dead metaphors of the lazy thinker. The word that first comes to mind about his teaching, as about himself, is vitality. His thought was intensely alive and vitalizing; it darted straight to the heart

[1] Manson, op. cit. pp. 5–56.

of the real issue; and he communicated it in language which, in its vigour and its inevitability,[1] has kindled the minds and imaginations of men and women everywhere ever since. Many of his phrases have become proverbial and are quoted by thousands who do not know who coined them.

The teaching was not delivered *in vacuo*. It was not, as it were, a continuous course of lectures enumerating general propositions. It was spoken to some one person, or group of persons, at some one particular occasion. (All true universality is bound up with concrete particularity of expression.) Therefore it does not all stand on the same level. One of the first steps towards understanding it is, therefore, so far as the evidence permits, to decide to whom and on what occasion the various sayings recorded in the Gospels, with few indications of time and place, were spoken. Admittedly, this will not be always possible. But Manson has shown, after exhaustive analysis, that there are three distinguishable groups, differing in background and outlook, to whom the remembered teaching was first addressed.

(*a*) There was the Rabbinic or learned world, the legal and theological experts who are found so frequently to be 'asking him questions'. Some were genuine requests for guidance. Out of all the vast corpus of the Torah, which is the commandment that really matters? How can belief in a life after death be squared with the law of the 'levirate' marriage? (Mark **12**. 18–26). Others, like 'tribute to Caesar', were probably traps. Jesus was addressed by them as 'Rabbi', acknowledged as a master in their own craft; and the antecedent probability is that he did engage with them in learned debate, not least on points of Scriptural exegesis (cf. Mark **12**. 25, 26).

In the fourth Gospel he is presented constantly in controversy with 'the Jews'. He may well have used very different language from that required for popular presentation, and this need not in itself be unhistorical. What the modern reader feels to be out of character is the note of stridency which has crept into it – an

[1] 'Consider the lilies, how they grow.' Substitute 'Take an analogy from the plants', and you won't have said the same thing at all.

echo, perhaps, of the strained relations between Church and Synagogue after his own lifetime.

(b) There was the intimate teaching delivered to the inner circle, 'the disciples', particularly the Twelve, to whom, especially after Peter's confession, he opened the secrets of his heart. (See the chapters on 'The Religion of Jesus' and 'The Son of Man'.) It should be noted here that the 'Great Sermon' was delivered, according both to Matthew (5. 1) and Luke (6. 20), to 'the disciples', not to the world in general.

(c) There was the public teaching to 'the multitude', the characteristic form of which was the parables, which have become a treasured part of the world's literature.

What is a parable? The Sunday-school answer ('an earthly story with a heavenly meaning') is inadequate if not positively misleading. It does not begin to do justice to these creations, which do *not*, on the face of them, have heavenly meanings. This answer is really descriptive of an 'allegory' and may lead to fatal misinterpretation; for that is just what a parable is not.

A parable is 'essentially an art-form capable of speaking in symbols to the human situation at any time'[1] and a highly developed literary art-form. It can be seen, as it were in the making, through the following stages in the use of symbolism.[2] A man may make a true but dull statement in terms of some such general proposition as that 'wealth can be a hindrance to virtue'. Moralists have been saying it since the world began, and though everyone knows that the sentiment is 'correct' it has never fired anyone's imagination. If, like a poet, he thinks in pictures and images, he may speak of the 'burden on a rich man's back', or say, like the Magnificat, that God 'has filled the hungry with good things and the rich he has sent empty away'. Or, in a picture still more vivid and memorable, he may describe the ridiculous attempts of a camel, the biggest animal known in Palestine, to squeeze itself, all humps and neck and hoofs, through the

[1] From a sensitive and very 'modern' study by Geraint Jones, *The Art and Truth of the Parables* (S.P.C.K., 1964).

[2] On this see C. H. Dodd, *The Parables of the Kingdom* (Nisbet, 1935), pp. 16ff.

eye of a needle – and that is what Jesus did.[1] (Camels seem to have fascinated him; cf. the mosquito and the camel in Matthew **23**. 24.)

Metaphors can further be built up and extended to form a sustained comparison or simile. Similes, the elaboration of images, are the highlights of some of the greatest poetry – for example, in Homer, in Virgil or in Milton (cf. the well-known 'Thick as autumnal leaves that strew the brooks in Vallombrosa ...').[2] Some of the 'parables' are really similes – 'The Kingdom of God is "like" a man, or a woman, who ...' This is a picture that throws light on the meaning of it.

Then, in the final form, what we may be given is a story, a piece of imaginative fiction, describing some particular situation which illustrates a whole world of experience, inviting the hearers to make up their minds about it and ask themselves what decision it requires of them. Nathan's story about the ewe lamb (2 Samuel **12**. 1–7) is an outstanding Old Testament example. This is what might be called the parable 'proper', like the Good Samaritan or the Prodigal Son. (These are what the German scholars call *Novellen*.) In the hands of Jesus, 'the thing became a trumpet'.[3]

But it is important to realize that a parable is not and is not intended to be an allegory. If it is allegorized it is ruined. In an allegory, such as *Pilgrim's Progress*, every detail in the narrative is designed to suggest an exactly corresponding spiritual counterpart or 'heavenly meaning'. In a parable, the details of the story are not meant to have any 'spiritual' significance, they are simply part of the story-teller's art, part of the machinery of the

---

[1] There is no ground for the suggestion that the needle's eye was a low gate in Jerusalem, nor that what he said was 'cable' not 'camel' (*Kamilos* for *Kamelos*).

[2] *Paradise Lost*, Book 1, 300–2.

[3] 'A story becomes a parable when it elaborates a pattern by which the story-teller intended to generate a cosmic disclosure. In one way or another a parable contrives to point to something. It does not just picture a state of affairs ... The story may be of 'the Sower' or 'a certain man', yet it must be such as possesses a structure repeated in situations the world over'. Ian Ramsey, *Christian Discourse* (O.U.P., 1965), p. 7.

story, making up the complete artistic whole. But, unfortunately, the parables of Jesus have too often been treated as though they were allegories (nothing will stop preachers from doing it!) and so submitted to fanciful and grotesque theological misinterpretations. That process began earlier than the Gospels. Inserted into the Gospels themselves are three allegorical interpretations of the Sower (Mark **4**. 13ff. and parallels), the Wheat and the Tares (Matthew **13**. 36ff.) and the Net (Matthew **13**. 47ff.) – it may be supposed that they were primitive sermons – which quite misrepresent their original purport.[1]

But this method, if pressed to its logical conclusion, leads to completely untenable positions. In the Unjust Steward story (Luke **16**. 1–13) for example, if the parable is treated as an allegory then 'the Lord' will be Jesus himself, or God, and we are left with Jesus (or God) 'commending' the unjust steward for being a rogue – which is hardly conducive to Christian morals! But all that is simply part of the story. The employer ('the Lord') says 'Well, that man was a rascal, but I must say he knew how to feather his own nest'. The whole story is leading up to the point that worldly people are often more alive to their interests than the religious are; the children of this world are, for their own purposes, wiser than the children of light. (The verses that follow read, as Dodd said somewhere, like alternative sketches for sermons on the parable.) So again in the story of the Wedding Feast (Matthew **22**. 1–14; Luke **14**. 15–22) the invited guests are depicted as so absorbed in their own immediate selfish interests that they forfeit the proffered invitation. That is all. The rest is simply part of the story. The details are not meant to be 'edifying', nor are 'heavenly meanings' meant to be extracted from them.

This broad principle of interpretation is applicable to the whole range of the parables. Yet every generation of Christians will rightly find their own meanings in them, and what they find, what the parables 'say' to them, is part of their inexhaustible meaning-content. There is 'yet more light and truth to break

[1] On this see the Commentaries and Dodd, op. cit. pp. 13, 14, 183, 184.

G

forth'. Not the least achievement of any great teacher is the response he evokes from his students. 'The Spirit,' promised the Christ of the fourth Gospel, 'shall take of mine and declare it unto you (**16.** 14).'

*   *   *

Yet right across the threshold of the parables, Mark has drawn a trail of mystification (Mark **4.** 11, 12; see the longer version in Matthew **13.** 10–16). Jesus is reported as having said that the reason why he taught 'those without' – that is, the general public – in parables was in order that they should not understand, and as though to guard some esoteric doctrine – 'the mysteries of the Kingdom of God'. It is hard to believe that he did say just that. Frankly, if we take it as a *verbatim* record, it would raise doubts about his mental health. Would a perfectly sane mind plan a course of teaching with the intention of not being understood? It is not easy to reconcile such an attitude with what we know of his outlook and his aims. Would Jesus treat his hearers with contempt, as people not to be trusted with his message? Surely the whole purpose of his ministry was to reveal and communicate the truth of God's Kingdom, not to conceal it.

As it stands, the passage appears to reflect a particular theory held by Mark himself – the theory of the Messianic Secret. Mark is concerned to insist that our Lord was 'designated' Messiah at his Baptism – not, as St. Paul said (Romans **1.** 4) by the Resurrection – but that men did not know that *and were not to know it*. During all his life in the world he was, as it were Messiah *incognito*; that was the mystery of the human life. We have seen already, and shall be seeing again, that Jesus made no public claim to Messiahship – if, indeed, he thought of himself as the Christ at all – and charged the disciples not to make him known. Deep theological questions are involved here. In point of fact the majority of the parables are not concerned with his own claims or status. (The Wicked Husbandman is no doubt an exception.) But it is extremely difficult to accept that he was deliberately speaking in order that people 'should not perceive'.

But the key to this very difficult position may be linguistic rather than theological. The passage in Mark is quoted from Isaiah (6. 9, 10), and there seems to have been a foreshortening in the perspective. The prophet received his commission at the great moment when he saw the Lord high and lifted up and heard the voice saying 'Who will go for us?' But the message that he delivered was rejected and, recalling the whole experience in retrospect, he speaks as though the message entrusted to him had been not simply one that was rejected but one that was given to him *to be* rejected. 'Go and say to this people, Hear ye indeed but understand not; and see ye indeed but perceive not' – he reads back what happened as result into the terms of the Call itself – 'lest they see with their eyes and hear with their ears' – i.e. in order that they shall not. A consecutive clause has thus become a final clause, and that is clearly the crux of the whole problem.

Well-supported scholarly opinion suggests that the solution may lie in the Greek mistranslation of the original. In the Targum, the passage from Isaiah runs 'who seeing do not see and hearing do not hear'; it is a relative, not a final clause. Accordingly, what Jesus may have said is, 'parables are for those who are without, who are people (i.e. because they are people) who seeing see but do not perceive; if they did see and hear they would repent'.[1] 'He that hath ears to hear, let him hear!' But the multitude did not 'hear', they did not really take in the message or understand what the Teacher intended. They needed stimulus and confrontation; what they needed was to be made to listen. (Cf. the opening of the 'Sower', 'Hearken!') This was the intention of the parables, the object of which was 'not to provide simple theological instruction, but to produce living religious faith'. Their interpretation, however, one by one, is too large a task for the limits of this book. Many excellent books are readily available. But a word must be added about the 'Ethical Teaching'.

[1] Manson, op. cit. pp. 74–80, and Dodd, pp. 13, 14. The idea that parables were meant to be esoteric lore may well have taken shape in a Hellenistic environment.

Jesus gave no ethical instruction, in the sense of a system of ethics or moral maxims which can be detached from the total whole of his teaching and stand independently of the rest. Everything he said about life and conduct issued from what he believed about God. His 'ethic' is essentially God-centred. There are no Christian ethics on any other terms. 'Morals', for Jesus, meant doing the will of God, on earth as it is in heaven. His concern was with the springs of motive rather than with particularized actions. What he offers is not a set of rules for conduct so much as a series of illustrations of the way in which a transformed or 'converted' character will express itself in positive acts and deeds. The Good Samaritan story, for example, was evoked by the question, Who is my neighbour? What are the limits of social obligation? The answer was not a lecture on Sociology but the picture of a character to admire. 'Go and do thou likewise' – but the man must decide just what that implied for himself.[1]

Jesus, accordingly, always refused to legislate. When asked to arbitrate over an inheritance, what he said, in effect, was, 'if it were not for covetousness, questions of this kind would not arise at all' – and this point he embodied in a story (Luke **12.** 13–21).

This was where he clashed with the Scribes and Pharisees, for whom the Law – that is, an external discipline – was the standard and safeguard of right conduct. As they sensed – and St. Paul afterwards said right out – his teaching meant 'the end of the Law'. The two great Commandments are absolute. 'There is no other commandment greater than these';[2] and these are not really 'commandments' at all, in the sense that they do not prescribe defined actions but concentrate on an inward disposition – that re-orientation of life and thought from the self as centre to God as centre, which is what he meant by repentance

[1] See my *Christian Ethics and Secular Society* (Hodder & Stoughton, 1966) ch. 4.

[2] Matthew's version, 'On these two commandments hang all the law and the prophets' (**22.** 40), brings back the whole corpus of the legal system as though they were derivative from that, and thus makes Christianity into a 'new law'. That indeed is how Matthew himself conceived it. But is this what Jesus had said, or meant?

('metanoia'). The precepts of the Sermon on the Mount are descriptions or illustrations of the ways in which such conversion will work out in practice. They are not legislation for a mixed society. They cannot be just 'applied', like paint or wallpaper.

14

THE RELIGION OF JESUS

I T is frequently remarked that Christianity is not the religion *of* Jesus Christ, the religion which he professed and practised, but the religion *about* Jesus Christ, the religion of which he is the centre. And that, say its critics, has been the big mistake – it has theologized him away from us. But, as I have been trying to point out, New Testament Christianity, both as a way of life and as creed and worship, grew out of Jesus Christ himself; and the Christian understanding of God derives from him and his understanding of God, that is from the religion *of* Jesus. The exalted Lord and Object of worship is the Lord portrayed for us in the Gospels, himself a profoundly religious man, conscious of his dependence on God. The Christian religion grows out of his religion and was from the beginning implicit in it.

There is very little in the recorded teaching of Jesus about 'religion' in its technical sense of specifically religious activities – indeed the word does not occur in the Gospels. He spoke about life and the right way of living it. His concern was not with religion in the narrow, modern meaning of the word, as one special department of experience, but with a total experience of life and an attitude to life as a whole – an attitude fundamentally religious. Religion is life experienced in depth, and Jesus lived in depth, at the heart of Being, where the springs of life come forth from Reality. His life reveals and communicates that Reality. To know Jesus is to know God. The Gospel is a Gospel about God; not about 'ideals' but about reality, the spiritual structure of the universe, what life means and how the world is made. That is what Christianity is about and that is what 'the divinity of Christ' implies. To the first believers this was self-evident: the Gospel was good news about God, and God was made known to them in Jesus Christ.

To our generation belief in God comes hardly, and indeed to many twentieth-century men the very idea of God has gone dead and seems to have neither validity nor significance. Can we not, they say, get on just as well without it? It is indeed in Christian circles that we are told that 'God is no more' and given books about 'the death of God'! To give the name God content and meaning is our supreme theological task today. That is what Christianity has always stood for – the knowledge of God 'in the face of Christ'. It is through him, as he lived and as he died, not only through the language he used, that the reality of God lays hold upon us.

His whole approach to life was God-centred. We might say that he sacramentalized life. Concerning his actual religious practice, little information has been preserved for us. Something is known of the circle from which he came and the influences under which he grew up, and presumably his prayer-life was moulded by them. The brethren must have been following his guidance in 'continuing steadfastly' (Acts 2. 46, R.V.) in public worship; and although he foresaw that it would be destroyed, he had a strong reverence for the Temple. It made him indignant that it should be profaned and turned into 'a den of thieves'. John says that he went up for the great Festivals, and quite certainly the Passover held deep meanings for him. We know, too, that he felt the necessity for periods of withdrawal and solitude, either in lonely, country places or in such privacy as he could get. 'Go into a room by yourself, shut the door, and pray to your Father who is there in the secret place' (Matthew 6. 6, N.E.B.).

We find no warrant in the life of Jesus for any 'religionless' Christianity (as that phrase is popularly misunderstood). But what, we must ask, did 'God' mean to him? For, as Canon Webster said lately, 'religionless Christianity is infinitely preferable to Christianless religion'. The characteristically Christian name for God is 'the Father of our Lord Jesus Christ'. This was the name which he had himself bequeathed, and St. Paul in an early letter (Galatians 4. 6) preserves it for us in the Aramaic which he had himself used – the authentic echo of his own voice. When he used that name, what did it mean to him?

The Fatherhood of God

Speakers at Mayoral banquets and similar functions often refer obliquely to Christianity as 'that sublime doctrine which teaches the Fatherhood of God and the brotherhood of men.' That, however, is not specifically Christian; and although Harnack maintained in a famous book that this is the essential content of the Gospel when 'stripped of its legendary accretions', it is not, in that form, what Jesus taught. It could mean merely that men have a common origin and are therefore members of one family. But that is no basis of spiritual brotherhood. (Members of a family often quarrel!) There *is* a sense in which it can be maintained that he stood for the religion of Humanity. But that is not what is meant by God's Fatherhood.

It was only when teaching his followers how to pray that he actually used the phrase 'Our Father'. And he seems to have spoken of God as Father always with a certain reserve, and with that mysterious indication of distance between himself and even his intimate friends which can often be felt so strongly in the Gospels (cf. 'My Father and your Father' – John **20.** 17). This suggests that it had a special meaning for him, and was used to describe an intuition or experience which was unique to himself; or, in other words, that the Christian knowledge of God is a knowledge mediated through him, a communication of his own experience.

Father is, no doubt, a word used of God in many religions, and notably in Judaism. Pagan faiths often spoke of God as Father in the sense of the physical progenitor of a hero, or a tribe or a city. The Old Testament uses the word in a special sense, denoting not only the Creator, Source and Owner of all the world and its peoples, but also as a moral and spiritual relationship. God was a Father unto Israel and Israel was God's chosen son (Hosea **11.** 1), not simply by physical descent but, as it were, by adoption and grace – by God's purpose and calling,

which was vindicated in the mighty act of deliverance from
Egypt, and verified in the covenant-relationship, which promised on God's side fatherly protection and entailed on their
side filial obedience.

In the Rabbinical teaching of our Lord's time the Fatherhood
of God was commonly spoken of, often on an exalted spiritual
level. It was not a phrase that Jesus invented or a revolutionary
new idea; it is found at all stages in the Scriptures and is still
central in Jewish thought today. But the Fatherhood of God in
the New Testament is 'not just a title or an article in a creed, but
a burning conviction, a spiritual experience which gave new
meaning and value to life and brought new joy and peace to
human hearts'. And it was through Jesus himself that this had
happened. 'What had he done to this common element in the
tradition which he had inherited to give it such power in the
lives of men bringing a peace that passes understanding?'[1]

*　　*　　*

A striking fact that emerges from the Synoptics is that, although the name and what it stood for to him is so utterly
characteristic of Jesus, yet it was but rarely that he spoke about
it. That is not, it is true, the impression that meets the eye. He
seems to be using the name from the beginning – one has only
to mention the Sermon on the Mount. But the Sermon is Matthew's composition, made up from sayings spoken at various
times, and we do not know at what stage in his life he uttered
them. Apart from that, it appears from a careful analysis that
in Mark and Q he speaks of the Father only in conversation
with the disciples, and after the turning point of the Ministry
the confession of Peter at Caesarea Philippi. (The only exception
is in Luke's special source [Luke 2. 49], when he was a boy, and
to his parents.) This was something that mattered to him so
much that he seems to have been unwilling to speak about it
except in the intimacy of the inner circle. To them he sought to
communicate what it meant to him and to train them in fuller
understanding.

[1] Manson.

This was indeed the holy of holies in the sanctuary of his own soul, the deepest truth in his spiritual experience. For him the word Father was 'not a dogma or a phrase of traditional piety, but a profound experience of the present living reality which pervaded and controlled his thought and actions'. It entailed a total trust and total obedience in a life totally freed from self-concern, and it gave him that sureness of touch, that courage, poise and inward serenity, and that independence of human judgements, which marked him out as a master of men. It was his entire dependence on the Father which made him the one perfectly free man.

He taught, people said, 'with authority, and not like the Scribes', who, being law-students, taught by the compilation of 'authorities' (Mark 1. 22). ('We speak that which we know and testify of that which we have seen' – John 3. 11; 'My teaching is not mine but his that sent me' – John 8. 14–16.) The prophets spoke with passionate conviction, claiming that the word which they uttered was not their own but had been *given* to them. 'Thus saith the Lord' was their credential. Jesus spoke as of right, in his own person, with an authoritative '*I* say unto you'. He moved among men with that same authority. The Roman centurion recognized a Commander: 'Speak the word only and my servant shall be healed' (Matthew 8. 8; Luke 7. 7). He called unto him 'whom he would', and they did not question his claim to their allegiance. By his presence he calmed the terrors of the 'possessed'. In the storm on the lake he alone remained unafraid – master in that, as in every situation – and, as they said, 'made the storm to cease'. He brought peace and order into the sick-room (Mark 5. 39, 40). Where he was, faith and hope revived. He evoked intense devotion and bitter hatred – in encounter with him nobody could be neutral. He loved children, and women brought their troubles to him; but armed troops sent to arrest him fell back.

Moreover, though the whole burden of his message was that men must be reconciled to God, he did not shrink from calling men to himself, and requiring from them a loyalty which can rightly be given only to what is absolute – so sure was he that in his words and deeds the Father was present and was being revealed. Something greater than the Temple is here (Matthew **12.** 6). 'He that receives me receives him that sent me' (Mark **9.** 37 and parallels). Without doubt he claimed to know God uniquely, in unparalleled intimacy and depth, and with a reciprocity that remained unbroken. 'No man knows the Father but the Son, no man knows the Son but the Father' (Matthew **11.** 27; Luke **10.** 22; Q). This was the central certainty of his life, too sacred to be discussed in public. To the inner circle of those who trusted him, however little they may have understood, he sought to communicate what it meant to him, so that they might be initiated into it and united in a spiritual brotherhood. 'One is your Father', 'One is your Teacher', and 'you are all brethren' (Matthew **23.** 8, 9).

In the teaching as recorded by St. John, the Father (or my Father) is central and is indeed the determinative phrase, so that for Christians it has become the 'natural' name for the Power that runs the universe – the Father of our Lord Jesus Christ. For St. John the Son is what Jesus essentially *is*. The words he spoke, he spoke not of himself ((**14.** 10); the works he did, the Father was working in him (**10.** 32). He is 'in' the Father and the Father 'in' him. To know the Son truly is to know the Father. That conviction Jesus had himself implanted. It was no mere theological proposition, but a vital experience which he had mediated. 'For him the Father was the supreme reality in the world and in his own life, and in his teaching he would make the Father have the same place and power in the lives of his disciples.'[1]

He did not validate that intuition in 'sacred' or technically 'religious' forms, or in terms of abstract definition, but in his whole interpretation of life and his response to life-situations. He was no ascetic like John the Baptist (Matthew **11.** 18, 19). He accepted life with gladness and reverence. He rejoiced in the lilies of the field. He saw God in the processes of nature and the 'secular' activities of men. He went out to dinner when he was invited. He was intensely vital and he loved life. His

[1] Manson, op. cit. p. 115.

determination to lay down his own life had nothing whatever to do with a death-wish – he could never have said, 'Welcome, Sister death'. Yet he lived in detachment from this world, in communion with the transcendent reality which he has taught Christians to call Father, sustained by unseen spiritual resources from which he derived the invincible conviction that the ultimate fact in the world, and in human life, is self-imparting Goodness and Love.

* * *

But *was it true*? Was it only a lovely dream? We are learning that the images we form of God are at best imperfect analogies, needing constant critical scrutiny and revision. People today are suspicious of 'father-figures', as symptoms, they say, of not being fully 'adult' nor brave enough to stand on one's own feet. Was the faith of Jesus no more than a 'projection' of man's hunger for spiritual security? Is the imagery of Fatherhood still valid? Must it not suggest an Old Man 'up there'? It is not the name which Jesus used for God, sacred though it has now become for Christians, on which human destiny depends, but the reality which he was intimating. At the core of his being was he right or wrong? What he had to say about his 'coming' was bound up with his belief in God, his certainty that the world is the kind of place in which he could come into his own and the cause for which he stood would be vindicated. Can a generation, hard-boiled and sceptical, with a non-personal, 'scientific' world-view, and bitterly disillusioned about life, really believe that the Power that runs the universe, the final truth about life itself, is disclosed to us 'in the Face of Christ'? That is the central question of our time, and on it the future of mankind depends.

Such a conclusion seems *a priori* improbable. Nobody, Christian or otherwise, can 'prove' it. We can only try to *learn* it from Jesus, by going with him into the place of prayer and by trying to follow him in the ways of life. What we mean by 'God', the God to whom Christians pray, is what 'Father' meant to Jesus Christ; and that implies a life-long discovery of its inexhaustible content and meaning.

People cry out in their agony and bewilderment. How *can* we believe that God is a loving Father when such terrible things happen in the world – Guernica, Auschwitz, Hiroshima – such cruel suffering falls upon the innocent? Yet Jesus called God Father while he was *on his Cross*. All this, of course, is part of the ultimate challenge to any belief in God – the problem of evil; and Christians have never supposed that it can be met except in terms of the Cross and Resurrection.

That was the core of the apostolic preaching, the centre of the good news about God, that he was indeed the God in whom Jesus believed.

Suppose that there really is a God like that, what should we expect him to care for most, what should we conceive that the world was created *for*? That men should be protected and kept safe from all accident and misadventure – treated like pet animals, as it has been put – or that character, that persons, should be perfected? Jesus employed the image of human parenthood as a valid analogy of God's providence. Which of you that is a father, if his son ask for bread, will give him a stone? (Matthew 7. 7–11; Luke 11. 9–13). Similarly, if a child asks to be brought up in a protected garden in which a maximum of pleasure and a minimum of pain is accepted as the supreme end of life, regardless of growth and development of character and of any but physical and material values – would a father who loved his child give it to him?[1]

Jesus put his faith to the final test, and the answer was the Resurrection. What was and is at stake in the Resurrection is not only belief in Jesus Christ himself, but the possibility of belief in God and so, at the end of the day, of belief in anything. But the world will not be won back to faith by repeating theological propositions. That can only happen by a revelation of Christ through a Church which is seen and felt to have something to offer which nothing else in this world can give – a communication of light and love and forgiveness in our darkness and loneliness and alienation. That is, in truth, what is meant by the Incarnation and Atonement.

---

[1] See Hick, *Evil and the God of Love* (Macmillan, 1966), p. 294.

110

The Man for others

As we have seen, the public work of Jesus was 'a ministry, not a demonstration'[1]. Jesus never said that he was 'God', nor was he trying to demonstrate that he was. Even in the theology of St. John, the mature Gospel of the Incarnation, the crude identification of popular orthodoxy by which Jesus himself has been obscured from us is carefully and deliberately avoided. He was not the Almighty. He lived as a human being. 'He that has seen me has seen the Father' (**14.** 9) is not to say 'I am the Father'. John presents him throughout as the Son, the One who perfectly knew and obeyed the Father, and that perfect union of thought and will is expressed in the saying 'I and the Father are one' (**10.** 30, *R.V.*). But union, however complete, is not identity. (Man and wife may be completely one, but that does not mean that the man *is* his wife.) Always, 'my Father is greater than I' (**14.** 28).

To say this is not to question the rightness of the later theological definitions when the Church had to formulate and defend its faith against 'heresies' that were incompatible with it. But it is to insist, and it needs to be said emphatically, that Jesus did not seek divine honours, nor did he seek to demonstrate his title to them. His aim was not to secure the recognition of his own status, to 'seek his own glory' – any such intention is altogether foreign to the mind of Christ – but 'to do the will of him that sent me', to serve God's purpose for the world.[2] He repudiated the compliments that were offered to him. 'Why call me "good"?' 'There is none good but God' – the self-imparting source of all goodness.

For himself he desired no honorific titles. If he were to disclaim his knowledge of God he would be 'a liar', false to what he was (John **8.** 55); but he received not glory from men (**5.** 41);

---

[1] E. Routley, *The Man for Others* (Peter Smith, 1965), p. 50.

[2] 'I believe that we are constantly in danger in our popular orthodoxy of paying to Jesus a regard which he expressly stated that he does not want, and withholding the honour which he does demand' – Routley, op. cit. p. 10. There is a good popular exposition of the orthodox 'Nicene' theology in ch. 6 of this book.

the glory he sought was the will of him that sent him (**7**. 18). Though he stood, as it were, on the Godward side of man, he stripped himself, not of his divine nature – he could only do that by ceasing to be himself – but of every attribution or title which might seem to separate him from humanity and suggest lordship or superior status. However the Church may formulate his divinity, it has never meant that he was a kind of superman. That would defy the evidence of the Gospels and would involve a denial of its own creed. He was made in all things like unto his brethren (Hebrews **2**. 17), bearing their griefs and carrying their infirmities, and at last tasting death 'for every man' (Hebrews **2**. 9).

He desired that men should hallow the name of God and glorify the Father who is in heaven. But that glory he revealed in ministry. To be God's Son was to be 'the Man for others' – to seek and to save that which was lost, as the shepherd seeks the lost sheep and the father runs out to meet the returning Prodigal. He appointed the Twelve to thrones in his Father's kingdom (Luke **22**. 30) but he taught them that royalty lies in service rendered; he that would be chief must be as he that serves (Mark **10**. 42–45 and parallels). 'I am among you,' he said, 'as he that serveth' (Luke **22**. 27). If the 'lord and master' had washed the disciples' feet, they should minister to one another as he had to them (John **13**. 14, 15). He came not to be served but to serve and to give his life a ransom for many (Mark **10**. 45).

For himself, he did not wish to be called Lord, Lord; that was not the way into the kingdom of heaven (Matthew **7**. 21; Luke **6**. 46, Q). He wanted men to do the things that he said. To believe in Jesus Christ does not mean only or primarily to use the same language that other believers use or have used about him. It means to obey, to set ourselves to follow, seeing in him the Way and the Truth and the Life. It implies a moral and spiritual decision. It was not what men called him that he cared about; it was whether they would be 'disciples in deed' and would follow the way that leads into true life (Matthew **7**. 14; Luke **13**. 24).

15

THE SON OF MAN

THE first believers called Jesus Lord and Christ – the most august title that they could give, the only title that, being Jews, they could give, to express the plenitude of his meaning for them – and it is of the Christ that the earthly story is told. There was bound to be some theological flashback in some of the stories told in the Gospels. For example, Mark and Luke both assert that the demons knew him to be the Christ (Mark **1.** 34 [see *R.V.* margin]; Luke **4.** 41). Some scholars would say that the story of Peter's confession embodies dogmatic truth rather than history. But in the Synoptics there is little evidence that Jesus applied the title Christ to himself.[1] That title, in popular Jewish expectation, was loaded with suggestions of temporal lordship, of power, dominion and conquest, which must have seemed to him to be incompatible with his understanding of his mission.

What he called himself was the Son of Man. This was his own self-chosen title; nobody else addressed him by that style, and the phrase does not recur in the New Testament anywhere outside the Gospels. In St. John **12.** 34 he is asked Who *is* the Son of Man? as though it was not immediately apparent that he was referring to himself at all.) It must surely reveal his own inmost thinking. Is it possible to discover what he intended by it?

Because it was his own chosen title, it was almost inevitable that the evangelists should represent him as using it on all occa-

[1] There are only three instances, Mark **9.** 41 (where Matthew **10.** 42 represents the original form) Matthew **23.** 10 and Luke **24.** 26, which quite clearly reflect early Christian theology – a suffering *Messiah* is not part of the O.T. tradition. At the trial before Caiaphas, according to Mark, Jesus accepts the designation (**14.** 61, 62); In Matthew (**26.** 63, 164) and Luke (**22.** 67) he is much less explicit. But in Mark and Matthew (not Luke) the whole emphasis of what he said is on the Son of Man.

sions. But here again careful analysis of the sources appears to yield evidence that he so described himself almost exclusively after Peter's confession and primarily, if not perhaps exclusively, in sayings about the Cross and Resurrection.[1] In Mark **8.** 38 and Matthew **10.** 23 it does not *explicitly* refer to himself. Matthew **11.** 19; Luke **7.** 34 is admittedly an exception.

The Son of Man is a Greek transliteration of the Aramaic phrase the-son-of-a-man, which, as it stands, means simply man. (This is a familiar semitic idiom, cf. Psalm **8.** 4, Man or the son of man.) That can be its meaning at some points in the Gospels, e.g. Mark **2.** 10 and 28. It could mean the man, this man, or in other words 'I' (so perhaps in Luke **7.** 34 (Matthew **11.** 19; Luke **11.** 30). But in applying the phrase to himself he was clearly using it in some special sense, and the whole probability, at least, is that this was derived from scriptural tradition. In the Old Testament, as in the 8th Psalm, the phrase denotes the prerogative of man, the dignity to which God has called him and his 'dominion' over the world of nature (Genesis **1.** 26) or, as we might say, man as essentially human, man as God intends him to be. In Jesus alone is human-ness fully realized; he is the one who reveals man to himself. But can he have called himself the 'ideal' man? There is something too self-conscious about that.

It is commonly assumed that Son of Man is a symbol of the human Jesus as Son of God stands for his divine nature. Most recent commentators, however, take it as the most exalted title in the Gospels, understanding by it the Son of Man in his heavenly origin and destiny as described in the vision in the Book of Daniel (7), one who would come on the clouds of heaven, and to whom there would be given dominion and glory and a kingdom. (It was this that Jesus was directly quoting in his final word to Caiaphas at the trial.) The theology of Mark, it has been maintained, is conceived in terms of a majestic paradox, 'that this glorious being, with God from the creation of the world, came to earth and was put to death . . . the supernatural connotations of the term are clear in Mark **8.** 38'.[2] But

---

[1] For detailed examination, see Manson, op. cit. pp. 211–36.
[2] F. C. Grant in *The Interpreter's Bible* (ad loc.).

H

the phrase as it is used in Daniel is highly coloured, figurative symbolism, and what the Son of Man means or stands for is 'the saints of the Most High' (7. 22), as the Beasts stand for the barbaric empires (7. 1–9). What the whole passage comes to is a prediction, in deliberately veiled and obscure language, of the victory of Israel and deliverance from the tyranny of Antiochus Epiphanes. 'The Son of Man has as much or as little reality as the Beasts which he supersedes.'[1]

But popular religious imagination had built up this figure of the Son of Man into a personal, more-than-human, deliverer, riding on the clouds to execute God's judgements and establish a new heaven and a new earth; and in the apocalyptic Book of Enoch, which may have appeared during our Lord's lifetime, this was further developed and elaborated. The Son of Man is a supernatural personage who would come from beyond this world in glory to possess all the kingdoms of the world and to be exalted into the presence of God. When such expectations were in the air it was inevitably suchlike images which would be aroused in the minds of his hearers when Jesus spoke about the Son of Man.

It is clear that they coloured the minds of the first Christians in their expectation of the 'second Coming'. How far, if at all, they coloured his own mind, it is not possible to determine. It has been held, notably by Schweitzer, that in fact they dominated his whole outlook, that his thought was through and through 'eschatological', that he expected a speedy end of history when he himself would come on the clouds of heaven, and that he died to make the dream come true. Undeniably there are certain passages, conspicuously the saying before Caiaphas, and perhaps the prediction in Mark 9. 1, which can be convincingly quoted in support of that.

But there is also a great deal in the Gospels which seems to point in a different direction. If the Son of Man, or Man, is lord of the Sabbath, there is nothing 'apocalyptic' there – no reference to Daniel or Enoch; it seems to mean Man as he is in the sight of God, or, as it has been put, 'a new type of man in whom God's purposes are to be fulfilled'. Support may be

[1] C. H. Dodd, *The Parables of the Kingdom*, p. 92.

claimed for this interpretation by St. Paul's language about the Second Adam. The first Adam is man spoiled by rebellion, the second is man remade in the image of God, and perfected man is manifested in Jesus (1 Corinthians **15**. 45). It may be that what Jesus had in mind was the Son of Man in the prophecies of Ezekiel – man 'standing upright on his feet' (Ezekiel **2**. 1), raised (that is) to his true human stature, the agent of God's purpose for the world, when he has been filled with the Spirit.

Majority opinion among scholars would, I think, tend to seek the origin of the Son of Man language in the Daniel passage, and to hold that the aim of Jesus was to revive or re-establish the 'saints of the Most High', the true and purified 'Remnant' of Israel. Some would go further and say that he used the title with a corporate rather than a personal reference. That still-to-be-realized people was the Son of Man. If that interpretation is accepted, it would involve that in his prediction about coming on the clouds of heaven he was thinking not of a personal glorification but, like Daniel, about the triumph of the saints – that is, the vindication of his cause. Or perhaps he identified himself with those whose destiny he represented and, as it were, personified in himself.

It is best not to try to define too closely the deep thoughts that were moving in his mind. What can be said with some confidence is this. As we have already seen, he conceived the true Israel latent in the people not as a saved but as a saving minority. But that saving mission involved suffering, as the Servant Songs had so wonderfully declared. But if so, if the faithful must be prepared for suffering, as he constantly warned them in his teaching, still more must the leader be prepared for it. There could be no room for a saved Messiah. He must lay down his own life for the sheep; and, as will be seen clearly in the next section, it is as Son of Man that he must suffer. Jesus did not die for his 'principles', he died for the salvation of his brethren.

I incline, therefore, to the view that the fundamental meaning of Son of Man is self-identification with humanity. He must die 'not for the nation only but that he might also gather together into one the children of God that are scattered abroad' (John

11. 32, [*R.V.*] cf. **10.** 16). For his message was essentially universalist – as Paul the pharisee was the first to realize. (See, for example, Luke **4.** 25ff., John **12.** 32). The vocation of Israel, which it had refused, was to be a light to the Gentiles; this one people had been chosen and trained to be the bearer of a worldwide mission. So then, the vocation of the saving remnant was to bring the knowledge of God to all mankind. Jesus worked within his own frame of time and place. He addressed himself to Israel, and told the apostles not to go beyond it (Matthew **10.** 5, 6, though this is in Matthew only and may be suspect). Let the children, he said, be fed first (Mark **7.** 27). Mark, and still more Luke, with their background, would clearly have been eager to present him as at work beyond the confines of Israel; but they were too faithful to the tradition to be able to indulge that desire.[1]

The ministry, which was for all the world, was concentrated in that one limited field. This is but one exemplification of the whole principle of the Incarnation, the so-called 'scandal of particularity'. No one can be mankind in general. Any real man must be that particular man. As Israel was Israel 'for the world', so he was that man 'for the sake of all mankind'. He stayed within the limiting conditions of the situation that God had ordained for him, accepting the necessary self-discipline. Yet he called himself the Son of Man rather than the Christ.

Son of David and Son of Abraham, he was, says Luke, no less Son of Adam (**3.** 38), representative of the human race. The same idea, if I am at all right, is latent in the title Son of Man. But it was as *this* Son of Man, as Jesus of Nazareth in his Jewish setting, that he brings salvation to men at all times and places. All he said was inevitably coloured by Biblical imagery and Jewish tradition, and the response it evoked from his contemporaries could not but clothe itself in those forms of thought. To

---

[1] Mark can only cite one incident, apart from the Roman Centurion at Capernaum, namely this one of the Syro-Phoenician woman (**7.** 24–30). His interest in the feeding of the 4,000, if it really is a separate incident and not a variant version of the 5,000, is probably that it occurred in pagan territory, in the hinterland of the Greek Ten Towns (Decapolis).

the first Christian believers he is the Christ, the goal and the fulfilment of history, as history is exhibited in the Bible. But all history belongs to God, and the revelation of God in Jesus Christ is therefore relevant to all history. It was a very orthodox Archbishop who said, 'It is an irony of history that since the first century the most familiar designation by his disciples has been Christ, and the religion which he founded has been called Christianity, rather than the religion of humanity, the religion of the Son of Man.'[1]

We cannot make Jesus a twentieth-century man. Yet he cannot be presented to the twentieth century in exclusively Biblical and Jewish terms, or he will not seem to be speaking to its condition. We have first to try to understand what was meant to those men in their own setting by what he said to them and what he was, and what the first believers were trying to say about him in terms of their Jewish background and tradition – and then to ask, What does it mean to us in a world so different from his and theirs?

It has been well said, in a very different context, that 'the artist must of necessity work with contemporary symbols, otherwise he has no means of communicating with his immediate audience . . . if he is an artist-journalist only that is [all] he has to offer, and in time he becomes a footnote. But if he is a serious artist he will infuse his immediate symbols with permanent and universal meaning; we will attach to them a significance greater than that of his times alone, which men of other times and places will be able to translate into their own terms and then appreciate . . . And if he is a great artist, he will bring himself consciously or otherwise into harmony with patterns of belief so old and basic that they form the ultimate stuff out of which meaning is derived; and it is to these ultimate patterns of belief that, in the final analysis, we respond, regardless of what [sic] other faiths (or faithlessnesses) to which we may be temporarily attached.'[2]

[1] J. H. Bernard, *Commentary on Fourth Gospel* (International Critical Commentary series) Int. p. xxxi, quoted by Duncan op. cit. pp. 273, 4.

[2] Weissinger: *Tragedy and the Paradox of the Fortunate Fall* (Routledge and Kegan Paul, 1963) pp. 9, 10.

*   *   *

The modern Christian ought to be told frankly that behind almost any statement in this section there is much debate and critical uncertainty. Some scholars, for example, question whether Jesus did call himself Son of Man. All these sayings they call 'community sayings' – that is, that they took shape in the early Church and were afterwards read back into the words of Jesus. Similarly, it is held by some that the incident at Caesarea Philippi is 'dogmatic rather than historical' – that it is a theological judgement read back and presented as actual narrative. In all this highly debatable territory I can only offer the reader that standpoint which appears to me to have most probability.

What seems to be certain, at any rate, is this – that as the early tradition took shape – and that must have been at first in Palestine – three different strands of thought become intertwined – Christ, Suffering Servant and Son of Man. This had, strictly speaking, no Biblical precedent; it was a Christian, not a Jewish fusion. The Biblical Messiah is Son of David ruling over a terrestrial kingdom – an idea which Jesus himself had rejected. The Old Testament knows of no suffering Messiah; the Christ on the Cross was to the Jews a scandal . . . (1 Corinthians 1. 23). The suggestion that a right reading of Scripture would show it behoved 'the Christ to suffer . . . and to enter into his glory' (Luke 24. 26) was what the Church had read back into the Scriptures; and this Christian re-interpretation of Scripture, interwoven with the Passion-narrative, makes it hard to discover from the Gospels exactly what Jesus himself taught. Yet this is the foundation-faith of the Church and the central content of the *Kerugma*. 'The fusion,' says Duncan, 'must be attributed either to the unfettered originality of Jesus in the interpretation of his mission, or to the faith which he succeeded in quickening in his disciples.'[1] Either way, it derives from the Lord himself.

This interweaving and fusion of Scriptural motifs is very clearly apparent in the Gospels at the crucial moment at Caesarea Philippi and in the story of the Transfiguration.

[1] Duncan, op. cit. p. 60.

16

WHO DO YOU SAY THAT I AM?

(Mark **8.** 27–33; Matthew **16.** 13–23; Luke **9.** 18–22)

I N the first Christian sermon, at Pentecost, Peter is reported
to have said 'God has made him both Lord and Christ, this
Jesus whom you crucified' (Acts **2.** 36). Even if he did not
actually say that, the words reflect the belief of the primitive
Church. In this story the post-Resurrection faith is carried back
into the Lord's own lifetime and expressed, appropriately, by
Peter. Here is the rock on which the Church is built. But what
is puzzling about the story is the attitude of Jesus himself. When
Peter makes the crucial confession his reaction seems to have
been the stern injunction not to let anybody know about it, and,
apparently, to reject the proffered title and to speak instead
about the Son of Man, whose impending Passion he now dis-
closes to his uncomprehending and resistant followers. Or has
the 'fusion' already occurred in his own mind?

The evangelists may have little sense of chronology, but Mark
seems definitely to regard the incident at Caesarea Philippi as
the critical turning-point of the Ministry, and Matthew to agree
with that placing of it. The Galilean Ministry is over, and henceforth the whole story is moving towards Jerusalem, heavy with
forebodings of tragedy, as the Son of Man goes to meet his
Passion, striding before them while they follow in fear (Mark
10. 32).[1]

The teaching now takes on a new note; he is saying new and
terrifying things about suffering as the cost of discipleship, about
the cup which he is destined to drink and the baptism with which
he must be baptized (Mark **10.** 35–45; Matthew **20.** 20–28); and

[1] 'John's design is circular, with the Risen Lord at the centre, whereas
Mark's is linear, with the Cross at the end' – Lord Eccles, *Halfway to
Faith* (Geoffrey Bles, 1966), p. 42.

it is increasingly addressed to the inner circle, especially the Twelve, whom he is preparing for what they must face.

The notion of a 'Galilean springtime', when the sun was shining and everything seemed to prosper, followed by a sense of failure and disillusionment, is a picture drawn by romantic imagination. From the very first there had been opposition. If there was 'failure', it was weeks and months ago, when the religious leaders had turned against him (Mark 3. 6). What would Jesus have called 'success' anyhow? The ground had been covered by 'primary evangelism'. The seed had been sown broadcast – how much of it had fallen on ground where it would bring forth fruit? The net had brought in an indiscriminate catch (Matthew **13.** 47) – how much of it would be useful for the Fisherman? The Apostles had carried the message round the countryside – how reliable was the response? Jesus was not the man to be taken in by the big congregation, the news-value, and the crowd that is always the backcloth of the Marcan scene. He needed to know whom he could trust, who was prepared to go with him the whole way, how much the Twelve, even, had understood or knew what it meant to be honoured with his confidence. Above all, what was their attitude to himself? Something like this must be what lies behind the question that strips the soul naked, Who am I?

In Mark the story is prefaced, perhaps designedly, by the healing of the blind man at Bethsaida ('men as trees walking'), as though to say that the ability to see by faith is a gift from God, 'sight to the inly blind'. This is one of the very few units in Mark which is not included in Matthew and/or Luke; to Matthew perhaps it was felt to be derogatory. An experimental healing, stage by stage, was more like clinical practice than a 'miraculous' cure by the word spoken. To us the story is very precious, reminding us that if faith has to grope its way 'through a glass darkly' through hesitations and doubts and fears, it is yet the True Light that lighteth every man who is guiding us all the time – we should not be seeking for him if he had not already found us.

Caesarea Philippi is in lonely country near the sources of

Jordan. It was built by the tetrarch Philip in honour of the reigning Caesar (in the Roman empire Caesareas were as common as Victorias in the British!) on the site of an ancient shrine of Pan. There Jesus asked Who do 'men' (i.e. the man in the street) say that I am? What is the popular belief about me? Some, they reported, say, like Antipas (Mark **6.** 14), John Baptist risen from the dead. Others say one of the major prophets. He was recognized as being no ordinary religious teacher, but someone outstanding and exceptional, to be appraised only in reverential categories. That was something but it was not enough. What depth, what commitment did it entail? He pressed nearer – And *you*, what do *you* say?

Jesus, it needs to be repeated here, had no interest in titles for himself. He cared little what people thought about him; what mattered to him was their response to God. This narrative makes us wonder whether he even thought of himself as the Christ. (Bultmann, who regards the whole story as fictitious, denies that he had any 'messianic consciousness'.) His one concern was that God's work should be done. But therefore he must know whom he could really count upon. For so urgent was the situation that those who were not for him were against him. Peter 'confesses' the faith of the Christian Church – Thou art the Christ. (Matthew has 'the Christ, the Son of the living God'; Luke, 'the Christ of God'.) Only the supreme Jewish title could do justice to what they had found in him or the faith and trust which he had awakened in them. Would that faith survive the Crucifixion?

Jesus was now recognized as Messiah (the Christ) *de facto* as well as *de jure*. If this was the recognition he was waiting for, surely he would thankfully accept it as a sign that the blessing of God was on his work. According to Matthew, *but Matthew only*, he does so, in a mood of great spiritual exaltation.[1] But in

[1] If the famous passage in Matthew 16. 17–19 is authentic – and it seems to depend only on M – it may safely be said that it does not mean what the power of the keys means in modern R.C. usage. Elsewhere in the Gospels (Matthew **28.** 18 and John **20.** 22, 23) the responsibility of 'binding and loosing' is committed corporately to the Apostles, i.e. to the Church as a whole, as the Body of Christ and the forgiving society.

Mark (and Luke) the only response is the strict command to silence. Was he refusing the title? Perhaps, as already suggested, he feared it as too much coloured with associations of temporal lordship and 'success'. And he may have been alarmed at the probable consequences of any popular messianic revolt, as he was after the feeding of the multitude (John **6.** 15). But whether or not he actually refused it, he began at once to break to them that his real mission (what he really *was*) implied still another way – that he must suffer. And it was as Son of Man that he must suffer.

Peter's protest springs from mixed motives. The first was a genuine misunderstanding; for what Jesus was saying cut across the whole inherited concept of Messiahship. The Christ must be a victorious, dominant figure – a 'saved' Messiah, not a suffering Saviour. And this touched Jesus himself very closely. It was the old temptation that he had rejected, now revived through one of his nearest friends, and a pressure to go back on that decision and betray his mission as he had accepted it. Hence the terrible 'Out of my sight, you Satan!' If Peter had still a great deal to learn, for Jesus, too, this was a crucial moment. Could he face the destiny of the Son of Man, and face it *alone*, with no understanding support?

But it seems clear that Peter was also thinking – as we all do – about his own prospects. What was going to happen to him and the other disciples? What place could they expect in the Kingdom now? What about the promotions and status they were hoping for? (cf. the story of the sons of Zebedee, trying to bargain for the senior offices – Mark **10.** 35ff. and parallels – which reveals our Lord's own attitude to 'status'). Might not some terrible fate, indeed, be awaiting them? For when Jesus spoke about taking up the cross, is it not possible that he meant it literally, as a corporate venture by his whole company, offering themselves to a redemptive death? When the time came none

---

The phrase about 'flesh and blood' may reflect the reply of the Syrian church (Antioch) on behalf of Peter to Paul's claim (Galatians **1.** 16) that he did not receive the Gospel by 'conferring with flesh and blood' (i.e. through any human agency) but direct from God by revelation.

of them could face it. In the garden he gave them their chance to escape – they took it – and offered his own life to save theirs (John **18.** 8; Mark **14.** 50). The Good Shepherd gave his life for the sheep.

But Peter's 'rebuke' showed that he and the others were still thinking in hopelessly worldly and 'sub-Christian' terms, thinking 'like men', said Jesus, 'and not like God'. (*R.S.V.* has 'not on the side of God but of men'.) From now on he is constantly unfolding to them what is meant in terms of cost by discipleship. (To suffer on Christ's behalf was Christian *privilege* – Acts **5.** 41; Colossians **1.** 24; 1 Peter **4.** 13–16 and *passim*.) It involved the surrender of all worldly prospects, it might demand 'forsaking father and mother', chopping off a hand or plucking out an eye, willingness even to lose life itself. The more he realized that he would be alone, the more clearly and dreadfully he realized that it was he who would have to accept the suffering, he who must be ready to lose his life to find it. The Crucifixion was a ghastly thing *inflicted* on him, agony and defeat, and his soul shrank from it in Gethsemane; yet all through the Gospels, and notably in the Fourth, there runs the insistence that he himself willed it (cf. John **10.** 18) and that though it was a supremely evil deed, the worst crime ever committed in history, and an outrage against God and man, yet nevertheless it was God's will that he should accept it as the price of Saviourhood. Here we begin to touch the profound mystery of the conquest of evil by his atoning death.

From now on, like the tolling of the bell, as someone has said, there sounds through the narrative the solemn, recurrent prediction of the Passion. Here some critical questions are unavoidable. For if the disclosure that the Son of Man must suffer was crystallized *at this stage* into these definite and precise predictions (including the rising again 'on the third day') as they are reiterated in the Gospels, then what actually happened is inexplicable. The disciples acted as though they had never been warned, had never been told anything about it; the arrest was a frightful shock and they ran away. (And, so far from 'expecting' the Resurrection and building up a gigantic wish-fulfilment, they refused to believe the reports when they came in.) Moreover, if Jesus himself had at this stage foreseen in this detail what was going to happen, it is hard for the modern reader not to feel that he was now acting a pre-determined rôle, knowing what was coming in the last Act, doing what he did because it was so 'written of him' (which is apparently what Matthew did think). But that seems to empty the facing of the Cross, when it came, of its moral and spiritual majesty, and to make of Jesus an automatic Redeemer.

The story of Gethsemane suggests that only then did he realize the issue quite definitely. What a terrible moral strain it involved for him – for the Cross could easily have been evaded. Probably no one would have been more relieved than Pontius Pilate if Jesus had gone underground. 'He saved others, himself he cannot save.' That was utterly true, but it was a moral, not a physical, impossibility.

We may say that these are predictions *post eventum*. But that is to say something more radical. It must be frankly recognized that in these sections the theology of the first Christian generation is colouring, and to some extent controlling, the presentation of the historical narrative.

So far from expecting the Crucifixion and being spiritually prepared to face it, the disciples broke – 'they all forsook him and fled'. We must always bear in mind that the Passion story, as it is related in the Gospels, is told from the other side of the Resurrection – that indeed is the meaning of the Transfiguration story – and seen in terms of a divine achievement. We must put ourselves back where his followers were then before they had any knowledge of the sequel. At the time it came to them as an appalling shock. All he stood for seemed to be repudiated; he was discredited and the cause was lost. There was no such God as he believed in. Their faith and hope had all been a ghastly mistake. One can hardly exaggerate their despair, their terror and numbing disillusionment – he had failed, and there was no God in heaven. (It is faithfully reflected in the Fourth Gospel, where they are seen huddled behind locked doors, and Peter says 'I am going back to the old job'. John **20**. 19; **21**. 3). It was a bitterly traumatic experience, made worse by the shame and guilt of their own desertion.

When he was restored to them in forgiveness – which is part of the meaning of the Resurrection, for the Christian Church was founded upon forgiveness[1] – then they had to try to understand and to make clear to themselves and to the Jews that the Cross had not been sheer blind disaster but was within the purpose of God; that Jesus had been delivered to wicked men and had been infamously done to death 'by the determinate counsel and foreknowledge of God' (Acts 2. 23). This, of course, must not be taken to mean that God willed the murder of an innocent man – that is inconsistent with Christ's revelation of God – but that God himself was nevertheless involved in it and through it worked out his purpose of salvation.

Any Christian approach to the mystery of the Cross, where the whole problem of evil is focused, must always be saying two things at once even though on the surface they are contradictory – that this was the worst deed ever done and man's most sinful rebellion against God, and that through it God brings healing and deliverance. That is the paradox of the 'Fortunate Fall'.

The believers therefore had to set themselves, being Jews with their roots in the Old Testament, to understand the Cross in the light of the Scripture, and Scripture in the light of the Cross. That is how Christian theology began. What was probably the earliest Christian document – it underlies all the books of the New Testament – was a collection of 'Testimonies' or prooftexts, showing that it had all been 'foretold' and that Jesus the Christ was the fulfilment of Scripture (cf. Acts 2; Luke 24. 27). He died for our sins 'according to the Scriptures' (1 Corinthians 15. 3). There are difficulties here for the modern Christian. Matthew, in particular, uses the Old Testament with a wooden and sometimes forced literalism which would not now be endorsed by competent scholarship, intent to show that things happened because they *had* to happen, because they had been 'foretold'

---

[1] C. H. Dodd, *History and the Gospel*, p. 158: 'The Church in its first utterances offered forgiveness to those who had killed the Lord.'

in the Bible.[1] But the prophets were not writing history back-
wards. The life and death of Jesus did not happen because they
were thus mechanically determined. We cannot use the argument quite as those men did. Some of the 'proofs' will not now
carry conviction. But in various forms the books of the Old
Testament (Psalms, Job, Ezekiel, Deutero-Isaiah) raise the ultimate questions of Faith in God – evil and suffering and death;
and Jesus answered them, he 'fulfilled' the Scriptures.

The Passion narrative in the Gospels is told in the light of that
scriptural exegesis, seeking deliberately to bring out what was,
or could be represented to be, the exact correspondence between the course it took and what had been foretold in the
prophets. It has thus a strongly theological interest. It reads like
a semi-liturgical composition, and may have been recited at
early Eucharists.

Dodd shows in his book *According to the Scriptures*,[2] how
deeply the mind of Jesus was influenced by certain Old Testament passages in particular. (If he has ever asked himself, What
Scriptures? the reader may be surprised at the list given.) How
far the early Church was guided in its interpretation of Scripture
by teaching given directly by Jesus, how far it may have attributed to him the words read out of its interpretation (e.g. Matthew **26**. 31; cf. Zechariah **13**. 7) are questions which cannot
now be answered. What is certain is that he reinterpreted the
traditional messianic expectations in terms of redemptive saviourhood through suffering, and because he accepted that as
God's will for him it was *necessary* that the Son of Man should
suffer (Mark **9**. 31). The necessity was in the loyalty of his own
will.

We tend to talk rather glibly about 'love' as though it were

---

[1] To take trivial, non-theological examples, Nazarene in Matthew **2**. 23
has really nothing whatever to do with Nazareth, and Jesus cannot have
ridden on two donkeys, Matthew **21**. 7. On the whole subject, see the
Introduction to Fenton's *St. Matthew* (Penguin).

[2] Nisbet, 1952, now in Fontana.

*   *   *

all that mattered in Christianity. But the 'new commandment' which Jesus gave is to 'love one another as I have loved you' (John 13. 34) and the true message of that love is the Cross. That was his most 'characteristic' action. We cannot think of Jesus apart from the Cross. That is why his death takes the place it does in Christian faith, experience and devotion.

17

THE TRANSFIGURATION

(Mark **9**. 2–8; Matthew **17**. 1–8; Luke **9**. 28–36)

T HE account of the Transfiguration presents the student
with many difficulties, alike of text and interpretation, as
to which readers must consult the commentaries. But the
central meaning and motif is clear enough, and for Christian
faith it is one of the most significant and revealing of all the
stories in the Gospels. It is the exaltation of the Son of Man.

Here the 'Lord and Christ' whom the Church knew, and as
it expected to see him at his 'coming', is revealed to these three
men, clothed in divine majesty in the light of a more than earthly
status and destiny. The Christian understanding of Scripture,
the Christian interpretation of Jesus himself – the answer of
faith to 'Who do you say that I am?' – is presented here as
having been continuous with his own self-disclosure during his
lifetime. That faith had been evoked by Jesus of Nazareth. It
was present, in germ, in what faith had then perceived in him –
as Peter had already borne witness.

Stories can communicate far more than can be conveyed by
verbal statements or by any theological proposition; and this
story is told about the human Jesus, who had toiled up over the
screes beside them and perhaps shared his lunch with them on
the way. It is Jesus in the days of his flesh who is the centre of
this revelation.

Some scholars have held that the evangelists have introduced
here, too early in their narrative, what was really one of the
Resurrection appearances, as Luke had apparently done in another instance (Luke **5**. 1–11; John **21**). But Mark's chronological note, 'after six days' (eight days in Luke) shows that he
put it here quite deliberately, as an epilogue to Caesarea Philippi.

The man to whom Peter had said 'Thou art the Christ' is seen
here in his predestined glory. It was more than an anticipated
glory. It was, as it were, inherent in his own person. In this man,
their friend, so humble and so mysterious, the glory of God had
even then been manifested. The Jesus whom they knew as man
among men is shown to them girt about with divine majesty,
'apparelled in celestial light'.

The details of the scene are richly laden with Old Testament
imagery and symbolism. In Exodus the mountain and the cloud
are the setting of divine theophanies; and the tent, the 'taber-
nacle', is the symbol of Jehovah's presence with his people
(Exodus **19**. 9; **24**. 15; Numbers **14**. 10; Revelation **21**. 1–3 –
when the Kingdom has come). (Mark says [v. 6, and Luke] that
Peter's remark about putting up tabernacles was phoney, but
there was much more to it than that.) In Jesus God had drawn
near to man.

'Transfigured' is the word used by Paul (2 Corinthians **3**. 18)
to describe the growth of the Christian in Christ-likeness. It
seems to suggest not simply that Jesus 'looked' different, his
face lit up and his garments glistened (no laundry could have
done the job, says Mark) – but some mysterious inward transformation through which an intuition was conveyed to them of
his true significance. They 'heard' the voice that he had heard
at his Baptism. They knew him to be the Son who revealed God.

Moses and Elijah, '*The Law and the Prophets*', bear witness
to him in whom they are fulfilled – he was the essential *meaning*
of the Scriptures, as the early Church was so much concerned
to emphasize. These two outstanding Old Testament figures had
both, it was written, seen God in theophanies, and both, according to Jewish tradition, had been 'translated', that is, had
not seen death. (They may be the Two Witnesses of Revelation
11. 3). That, however, is not what the Resurrection means.
Jesus did not escape death, he conquered it.

Mark's instinct in placing the incident here was quite right.
The fundamental meaning of the story depends on the place it
occupies in the narrative, between Peter's confession and the
Passion. Although Peter had acclaimed the Christ, he was

I

'thinking like a man and not like God'. He was still thinking that the divine majesty must be manifested in irresistible power, as though God were a kind of celestial Caesar; and too many Christians think like that still. Jesus was telling them that 'almighty power' is declared 'most chiefly in showing mercy and pity'.[1]

On the mountain the Son of Man who must suffer is seen transfigured with divine glory. Authority is grounded in love – that is what Christianity is about. The supreme revelation of the divine glory is seen in the way of suffering and humility.

As St. John was to say, the Cross *was* the glory (John **13.** 31). It is in what seemed like failure and defeat that Christian faith has uniquely found God and has learnt to say 'So God loved the world'. They understood that after the Resurrection; and so, as this story lets us understand, when the Gospels come to the events of Holy Week, they are not telling the story of a martyrdom but the Passion of the Risen Christ. The Cross was not a defeat, it was a conquest. Luke makes the connection explicit when he says (in the Greek) that Moses and Elijah were speaking to Jesus about his 'Exodus' – that new and mighty act of deliverance, which he was to accomplish at Jerusalem (Luke **9.** 31), giving his life as the price of the world's freedom.

It is no good asking what actually happened. Only the chosen three were present. Nobody else who was there would have seen anything, any more than a casual spectator would have seen anything at the Resurrection or when he 'ascended into heaven'. He was seen only by those who knew and loved him. It may truly be said that the Resurrection and exaltation 'at the right hand of God' – of which this story is a kind of foretaste – is something known only to the Church – though it can be verified by secular history. Who Jesus *is*, is known only to those who trust him. ('The love of Jesus, what it is, none but his loved ones know.')

*   *   *

'It is good for us to be here', let us stay. Always we want to

[1] *Book of Common Prayer*, Collect for Trinity 11.

hold on to the great moments, not to let them fade into the common day. If we could live permanently on the mountain-top, in the moments of awareness of God! But the rhythm of Christian life is from the peak to the dusty level plain of routine duty. For Christians there must always be this tension between the vision of God and the claims of the secular, *in which* it is to be obeyed and validated. Jesus and the disciples come down to encounter all the strains and confusions of an acutely distressing case of epilepsy. Jesus as the revealer of God must be identified with human need. 'Where mercy, love and pity dwell there God is dwelling too.' What he said to them about prayer and fasting gives us a glimpse of the self-discipline and depth of interior spiritual life which were part of the secret of his 'mighty works'.

18

RANSOM FOR MANY

(Mark 10. 45)

From now on, the story is moving towards Jerusalem and the great drama of the Liberation. He gave his life 'a ransom for many' – that is, as the price of delivering man from slavery. His career seems to be prematurely cut short and all his hopes to be overwhelmed in ruin. Yet the Cross was indeed the climax of his life and the place where supremely he revealed God. The New Testament and the faith of Christians see in the events of the Passion not merely something that men did to Jesus but something that God himself was doing, his uniquely redemptive action in history. It finds in them therefore a cosmic significance, the victory of light over darkness, of the Kingdom of God over the reign of Satan, the emancipation of man from the power of evil and all that threatens destruction to personal life.

The 'holy week' is the centre of history. Something was done then, Christian faith affirms, which has changed the whole human situation and brought man into new relationship with God. For all Christians, of all traditions and communions, the Cross is the centre of our faith and hope, the guarantee of the divine forgiveness by which we are set free from the burden of guilt and emancipated from the house of bondage into the glorious liberty of the children of God. Here we touch the central mystery of the story; what is commonly called the atoning work of Christ. Why did Jesus Christ have to die? And how can a death which happened two thousand years ago bring 'salvation' to twentieth-century men?

Even to begin an attempt to answer would involve theological discussions which are quite outside the range of a book like this. We can be concerned here only with the Gospels or other New Testament material. Yet if we cut the theology altogether we shall be excluding ourselves in advance from any understanding of the Gospel as the first believers accepted it – the Gospel which, as I have so often emphasized, is proclaimed through the narrative of the Gospels. We shall come back to this in a later paragraph. For the moment, what needs to be insisted upon is that Cross and Resurrection go together. As there could be no Easter without Good Friday, so there could be no Good Friday without Easter. It would be Black Friday but for the Resurrection. The latter is *presupposed* in the Passion narratives, which would never have been told if it had not happened. The Cross is the symbol of victory, not of defeat.

*   *   *

The week opens with the triumphal entry (Jesus's one deliberately planned 'effect') when he rode into the city – not on a charger, like a Caesar or military conqueror, but in the royal majesty of the Servant 'meek and riding upon an ass' – to claim the City of God for God's kingdom. Just what he expected to happen we cannot now know. Did he hope that he would be welcomed as the Coming One? Surely he saw too deep into human character – he knew, says the Fourth Gospel, what was in man (John 2. 25) – to entertain any such easy optimism. Jerusalem had always killed the prophets, always failed its vocation and its opportunities – the thought moved him not to indignation but to tears of pity – and would it not treat him in the same way? And of that he had time after time warned his followers.

The high probability, at the least, seems to be that he came to the city fully aware that it would cost his life, and resolved to offer his life for the people of God, because he believed that it was the Father's will and his vocation as the anointed Son. ('He sacrificed himself as Jesus,' someone has put it, 'to himself as Christ.') That a man should lay down his life for his enemies – there can be no greater love than that. Here was the divine quality of life revealed within the conditions of human life; and here is the encounter between God and the 'demonic' element in history.

Man is always in rebellion against God,[1] and all history, even at its best, is always bedevilled with the will to power. Jewish patriotism was in itself good; Jewish religion and Roman justice were the best religion and justice the world had known – and the Crucifixion was what they did. The Cross, as St. Paul was to put it, had shown up the exceeding sinfulness of sin. The world and the Church, involved in the world and in worldly values, are under Christ's judgement. 'Now is the judgement of this world: now shall the prince of this world be cast out' (John 12. 31). This is part of what is meant by the 'wrath' of God – holiness is reaction against wickedness. But God's reaction was not to descend from heaven in angry vengeance, like Zeus with his thunderbolts,[2] but himself (using human language) to become involved in the contradictions of history, overcoming evil with good, identifying himself with his world even in its wickedness and folly. Not even in its darkest hour was the world abandoned or God-forsaken. When we speak about Incarnation and Atonement we mean something like that or, at least, not less than that.

On Palm Sunday *Vexilla Regis prodeunt*. The King of glory passes on his way – and the way is leading forward to Calvary. The first act is the cleansing of the Temple, where commercial traffic was being made out of the word of God; and this was an open challenge to the Hierarchy, like Luther's theses nailed on the church at Wittenberg. There follow three days spent in debate and controversy, culminating in the so-called Day of Questioning. It may be thought antecedently improbable that all these confrontations and arguments were in fact crowded into so short a time. Various incidents have been massed together to exhibit his clash with the leaders of public life, representing

---

[1] 'Man is always trying to forget that he is up against God, and that what we are up against when we are "up against it" is God' – H. Richard Niebuhr, *Christ and Culture* (Faber 1952).

[2] In spite of the awesome Michelangelo mural on the East wall of the Sistine chapel!

many different opinions, but united in their resolve to get rid of him, and to build up the sense of mounting tragedy as the drama moves forward to the last act. Night by night he was fortified and sustained by the home-life of his friends at Bethany,

Judas defected and the net closed round him, but everything had been thought out and prepared. He made no attempt to disguise his whereabouts. (When the troops were actually on the way he went to the Garden 'where he often resorted' and where government agents would naturally look for him.) He needed the spiritual strength which he would draw from joining in the Passover, the commemoration of the great Deliverance from slavery and oppression into freedom, now to be re-enacted, as he believed, by the sacrificial offering of his own life. But would there be time to eat before he suffered? (Luke **22**. 15, 16.) The Upper Room had already been arranged for, and there he gathered the Twelve for the Last Supper.

There are chronological difficulties at this point which, though religiously of no real importance, split Christian churches for long years in controversies over the date of Easter. (What *have* Christians been doing with Christ's religion?) Was the meal in the Upper Room an actual Passover, as Mark apparently means us to understand, or was Jesus killed on the day when the lambs were slaughtered (14th Nisan), as the time-scheme in the Fourth Gospel indicates? (In Mark, the authorities say 'not on the feast day' (**14**. 2), which, however, is what they then proceed to do. Our liturgical sequence may have been over-simplified.)

On the whole, the tendency of scholarship seems now to be to endorse St. John's chronology, and support for it may be found in St. Paul's phrase 'Christ our passover is sacrificed for us' (1 Corinthians **5**. 7).[1] In either case, it is clear that in the Lord's mind the Supper was his own final Passover ('I will not drink again of this fruit of the vine . . .') and that in it he was identifying himself with the Reality which the ritual symbolized. This loaf, broken and shared, is my Body, this cup is my Blood of the new Covenant. (Christians have since been roasted over slow

[1] cf. Easter Anthem in the *Book of Common Prayer*, in the Preface, 'the very Paschal Lamb which was offered for us'.

fires for 'heretical' views on the meaning of the copula. And indeed too often Western Christianity, with the Latin legal genius behind it, has been hardened, narrowed and disrupted by attempts to define indefinables and to treat symbols as though they were factual statements.)

John does not record the 'words of institution'. In their place he relates the story of the foot-washing, as though to say Do *this* in remembrance of me. (The *earliest* form of the words is most probably that of 1 Corinthians **11.** 23–25, which St. Paul says he received from the Lord, that is, from the Palestinian believers, some of whom must actually have been present. The use in the Western liturgies is a conflation, introducing 'for the remission of sins' from Matthew **26.** 28). John had developed his eucharistic theology in connection with the feeding of the five thousand (John **6**).

The vital importance of this scene for the evangelists is that here is the origin of the Eucharist, the central point of the worshipping community created by the Cross and Resurrection, the distinctive mark of the Christian society and the acted truth of what the Church is and means. Right from the day of Pentecost until now, everywhere in substantially the same form, those who believe in Christ have met together on the first day of the week to break the bread – no other society in the world does that – in thankful remembrance of his death, to be 'raised' by him into newness of life and be made 'partakers of his resurrection'. All Christian experience corroborates, whatever the theological 'explanations', that here the Risen Christ whom the Church knows – the remembered Jesus who was crucified – communicates himself to his own in forgiveness, renewal and gifts of ministry; that through their fellowship with one another redemptive power may flow out into the world.

Straight from the Supper he led them into the Garden, to make his final, agonized, decision. (He must have seen many crucifixions, and he knew with terrible clarity what it meant. He loved life and he dreaded death – and such a death. But what more was there to cause his 'amazement'? Had the defection of Judas shaken him? Was the thought of man's hatred and wickedness and the sin of the world – God's world – too unbearable? Was there a dreadful moment, even now, when he wondered whether he had deceived himself and misinterpreted the Father's will?) He rose from prayer with his resolution steadfast and went forth serenely to meet the traitor. Henceforth he ceased to be, physically, a free agent. Yet the few hours that were left to him on earth were the decisive hours of his whole ministry.

*   *   *

We are not 'saved' by the physical death of Jesus but by himself, living, dying and rising again; and the Cross must not be regarded in isolation from what went before it and what followed after. The whole ministry of Jesus, as we have seen, was a ministry of reconciliation – healing the contradictions of human life, offering the franchise of forgiveness, bringing God near into the lives of men. ('Atonement' means reconciliation.) His death was its climax and fulfilment. Vast superstructures of theological doctrine have been built up in the course of Christian history in explanation of his atoning death. Some of these are, it must be frankly recognized, morally repugnant to the Christian conscience and irreconcilable with the revelation of God which Jesus brings to us. He did not buy off the anger of an offended God. He was not reconciling God to the world. God was in Christ, as St. Paul said, reconciling the world to himself. The Cross did not change God's attitude to mankind, it revealed what it always is and always has been. Other theories, dependent on the Fall story and treating an ancient myth as factual history, are now for the modern Christian inconsistent with any responsible attitude to the new knowledge brought by natural science and anthropology. They are none of them obligatory or *de fide*. None of them are in the Gospels or in the Creeds, which confine themselves to the narrative of the events.

There is no official doctrine of Atonement. And if, as it seems to many Christians now, the traditional doctrines have run into a *cul-de sac* we are free to explore some new ways of approach. The fact is greater than all the explanations. The new ways may prove to be the more ancient ways. We must clear our minds of all the accumulation of ideas about a juridical transaction between Christ and an offended deity, or between God the Father and God the Son, such as have been imported by later generations. ('There was no other good enough to pay the price of sin' – that brings in penal and judicial notions where personal categories are most essential. Only he could be the liberator who was himself inwardly free.) We must start more humbly and experimentally from the spiritual experience of Christians and return to the thought and language of Scripture and to the words and acts of the Lord himself.[1]

It must not be forgotten that Scriptural language – and this is true of much in Jesus's own teaching – is the language of metaphor and symbol. Confusion and misunderstanding has arisen through taking metaphors as factual statements and pressing them to their logical conclusions. Thus he spoke of his death as a 'ransom for many'. Before long, theologians started asking, To whom then was the ransom paid? Some said, to the Devil, others said later, to God; and vast consequential theories were elaborated! But such metaphors can be at best but pointers to a mystery which transcends all our logic.

In the Gospels and the New Testament as a whole two main roads of approach may be traced – the conquest of evil and reconciliation.

Mark exhibits the Ministry, as we have seen, as perpetual conflict with the powers of evil, personified in the demons. The Cross was the final encounter and the victory. The conflict of

[1] 'Those who theologized about the Atonement would have done better if they had realized the significance and logical status of the metaphors . . . which they used. In the event, it was their inordinate affection for descriptive language which led them not only into logical blunders but into Christian scandals.' For example, How does the Cross make us unrighteous, or How does the Blood effect Justification? Later thinkers became 'oblivious to the logical impropriety of such questions, so that the Blood is pictured in some causal, quasi-scientific fashion, as bringing about a change of state, people began to speak of a change in man's condition from a "state of sin" to a state of righteousness.' – Ian Ramsey, *Christian Discourse, some logical explorations* (O.U.P., 1966), pp. 29, 31.

good and evil in human hearts is part of the great cosmic war-
fare between life and destruction, chaos and order, light and
darkness, meaning and meaninglessness. In the Cross, St. Paul
said, the powers of evil, the world-rulers of this darkness, have
been broken, stripped of their empire and led in triumph as
captives (Colossians 2. 15). We may prefer to use different
language, and to speak of personality disorders, phobias, com-
plexes, the will to power. But the evil and its tyranny is still
there. Christianity offers no theoretical answer to the problem
of evil in God's world; it tells us how to meet it and overcome
it. The whole problem is focused in the Cross. Everything that
is worst in human nature was concentrated against Christ to
destroy him. Here are Good and Evil in stark confrontation.
They broke his body and laid his cause in ruins. What they could
not do was to defile his soul. The last word is with Holiness and
Love. God is mightier than the Devil. Jesus met his dreadful
pain not in protest, resentment or self-pity, but as the means
to spiritual victory; turning evil into the substance of greater
good. The essential meaning of Sin is the will to power – self-
assertion against God and Man. Purged from every trace of
self-concern, identifying himself with human need, and his will
in perfect obedience to God's will, he overcame not 'sins' but
sin in itself. He had taken away the sin of the world.[1]

'God commends his love to us,' St. Paul said, 'in that while
we were yet sinners Christ died for us' (Romans 5. 8). He died,
says Peter, 'The just for the unjust, that he might bring us to
God' (1 Peter 3. 18). Not by any lawcourt procedures, but by
bringing God near to sinful men. God does not withhold his forgiveness until we are fit or 'deserve' to be forgiven – we never
'deserve' benefits from God and no 'works' of ours can ever
earn them; he forgives men and accepts them as they are. That
had been a constant theme in the teaching of Jesus. As on the
Cross he prayed for his murderers, caring for those who were

---

[1] It means much more than this, but at least this. For an attempt at a
rather fuller discussion see my *Questioning Faith*. chs. 7 and 8, and a
forthcoming study, *The Atonement* (Hodder & Stoughton) in which I
have tried to go into it more deeply.

torturing him to death, so does God care. So God loves the world. The Cross is the good news of forgiveness, and the most creative work of Jesus Christ in the human heart is the forgiving spirit, which is the source of all true community.

When men in their estrangement and sinfulness know that they are accepted by God, then they are able to accept themselves, and being made whole, released from their inward conflicts, purged of the separating will to power, they may have fellowship with one another. That was what happened in the new *Koinonia*, the Community of the Holy Spirit, created by the Cross and Resurrection. That is where the atoning work of Christ is verified.

Christ, in St. Paul's words, had 'killed the enmity' and broken down the dividing wall of partition. The barriers of estrangement were down. The reconciliation had been achieved. As he died, he said, 'It has been accomplished.' The Resurrection is not merely a happy ending, a reversal of fortune before the curtain falls; it *crowns* the victory which had been won already.

As we must not isolate the Cross from the life of which it was the climax, so neither must we from what followed from it. It is in that total complex of events – his life and death, Easter and Pentecost, that there is for faith a unique revelation of God, a unique mediation of his redemptive power.

19

HE ROSE AGAIN ACCORDING TO THE SCRIPTURES

WHAT we cannot do is to say 'I accept the story in the Gospels as a reliable account of Jesus; they give a consistent and convincing portrait, and on the strength of it I can believe in him as the Way, the Truth and the Life. But when they add to it the super-miracle of the Resurrection and the empty tomb, there I hesitate, there I suspend judgement. The rest would stand even if that were cut out'. We cannot do that, because the Resurrection, as we have seen so often in this book, is what the Gospel story is *about*. It is taken for granted all through the narratives and not least, as I said above, in the Passion narrative. The story that the Gospels are telling is that of the earthly life of the Risen Christ. As Lord Eccles, who does not quite believe in it, has seen, 'the Gospels insist that the Resurrection is the central fact of Christianity'.[1]

Some Christians and would-be Christians regard it as an optional extra for Christian faith; some, like Bultmann, deny it altogether. This was, they think, a myth, a legendary accretion, built up by subsequent Christian devotion, not something that actually occurred. Yet Christianity, they say, does not depend upon it; the principles, the ideals, still remain even if the Resurrection did not happen. This implies a complete misunderstanding of the nature of Christianity itself, which rests not on principles or ideals but on 'given' historical events; not on a philosophy, but on a Person, who, as it affirms, 'for our sakes died and rose again'. If these events, including the Resurrection, did not happen, 'our preaching is vain and your faith is vain'. Christianity, then, would rest on a mistake.

[1] op. cit. p. 94.

The obstacle to belief, for the modern man, is that it 'violates the laws of nature' and is therefore something that could not have happened. But the 'laws' of nature, as I have pointed out, are only statistical generalizations, and a single negative instance disproves them – the exception proves (i.e. tests) the rule. The Resurrection, if it occurred at all, is *ex hypothesi* a unique event. It cannot be brought under any known 'laws' and compared with other events of the same kind, for there are no other events of the same kind; if there were, it would not be unique. The question is not whether it 'could' have happened on *a priori* ground, but whether it did happen. How strong is the evidence in support of it?

St. Paul appeals to eye-witness evidence (1 Corinthians 15) and his is, of course, the earliest account of the post-Resurrection 'appearances'. It may not be easy to square St. Paul's list exactly with those recorded in the Gospels. Harmonistic methods are now rightly suspect. There were clearly two streams of tradition, the one (Mark and Matthew) centred in Galilee, the other (Luke and John) in Jerusalem. They were told not to depart from Jerusalem (Luke 24. 49); they were told to go and meet him in Galilee (Matthew 28. 7). John's epilogue (John 21) brings in the Galilean tradition at the end.

Attempts are made to arrange all the records of appearances in a temporal sequence. But timeless realities have no temporal sequence – the Risen Christ is not in space/time – and we should perhaps hesitate to 'date' the appearances, or the Resurrection itself. The appearances could have been all simultaneous. St. Paul seems to attribute the 'third day' not to eye-witnesses but to 'the Scriptures'. The reference is probably to Hosea; 'after two days will he revive us: the third day he will raise us up' (Hosea 6. 1, 2), 'after two days' meaning soon, or in a short time. But it was apparently on the third day, i.e. on what we call Easter Sunday, which was 'after two days' by Jewish reckoning, that he was first 'seen' by Mary Magdalen – in other words, that was the 'date' of the first discovery. So it came to be held that he rose 'on the third day'.

Were these appearances 'visions'? Of course they were visions.

He would not have 'appeared' if he had not been 'seen'.[1] There is no need to be afraid of that word or accuse those who use it of 'selling the pass'. But if 'visions', could they not have been hallucinations? We need not rule out that they may have objectified an inward experience in visual form – a commonplace in the psychology of religion. But was it an experience of reality? Had the risen Christ really, objectively, presented himself to them as alive? *Had* they 'seen' him, or were they self-deceived? There is no suggestion of mass-hallucination or of any of the workings of crowd-psychology; and, as we have noted above the visions were certainly not the creations of wishful thinking. The Apostles were brought to conviction in spite of themselves, under the coercion of irresistible evidence. Something happened – this is incontrovertible – to change broken and disillusioned men, whose faith had been shattered when Jesus died, into Christian believers and evangelists, men who risked their lives for the 'good news', men who turned the world upside down. *What* had happened? They said that the Lord had risen. It is up to the non-believer to provide any plausible alternative explanation.

Christian faith does not ultimately depend on the discovery of the empty tomb. That was what brought conviction to Mary Magdalen and (according to John) to the two Apostles. Christianity does not depend on any theory about what happened to the Lord's body.[2] Most Christians believe that it came forth from the grave as the glorified organ of his deathless spirit and

[1] St. Paul, we notice, put his own experience on the Damascus Road in the same series as the appearances to Peter and the others.

[2] Professor Lampe, in a recently published book (*The Resurrection*, by Lampe and Mackinnon [Mowbray, 1967]), regards the story as having been gradually built up in the developing tradition rather than as a primitive element in it, and concludes, 'I regard the story as a myth rather than literal history, and profoundly significant as a myth.' (For the meaning of 'myth' in current theological usage see below.) A great deal of new thinking about the Resurrection and its significance for Christian faith and experience is now going on in theological circles. An exploration in depth of some of these themes the reader will find, to his great advantage, in the book mentioned. See also a set of articles in *Theology* for March 1967 (S.P.C.K.).

the instrument of his self-communication. And this, difficult though it may be on other grounds, is the most direct and simplest interpretation of the story preserved in all forms of the tradition, and is clearly how John means it to be interpreted. But no particular theory is *de fide* – the Creed merely affirms that he rose again.

There are two truths here, apparently opposed but in fact complementary, to be safeguarded. (1) By the Resurrection Christians do not mean the resuscitation of a corpse. In spite of much traditional preaching and teaching, this is not an event of the same kind as the raising of Lazarus or the widow's son. They had to die again later on. But 'Christ being raised from the dead dieth no more, death has no more dominion over him' (Romans **6.** 9). This belongs to the realm of spirit and personality, and is not contained within space/time limitations. (2) Nor do we know anything of disembodied personality, and the Risen Christ was not a 'ghost' (Luke **24.** 39). His risen life was continuous with his earthly life (cf. the wounds in John **20.** 24ff. and the meals in Luke **24** and Acts **10.** 41) even though there was real discontinuity. Christians do not mean that his 'soul' was immortal, or that though he was crucified, dead and buried he yet 'lives on' in influence and memory. This was not a survival, it was a conquest. It is not that Jesus somehow 'survived' but that he transcended and 'overcame' death.

Christianity rests on the conviction that he himself is personally alive, present in the Church and in the world, exercising his redemptive power and communicating himself to the hearts of men.[1] He is himself the Source of the 'risen' life.

No press photographers would have seen him rise. The Roman journals knew nothing at all about it. This was not, as it were, a public event. He appeared, said Peter, only to chosen witnesses (Acts **10.** 41). His presence was recognized by faith and love.

Yet it was a public event, in the sense that it 'was not done in a corner' (Acts **26.** 26). The events on which Christian faith is founded took place in the stream of public, secular history.

[1] See my *Questioning Faith*, p. 198.

Christianity therefore must not deprecate, and indeed should be eager to invite, the fullest historical investigation. Secular history can never 'prove' that Jesus Christ rose from the dead. All it can do is to show that a body of Jews who had been disciples of Jesus of Nazareth became convinced that he was alive, and that this conviction had momentous consequences in the development of Western history. If he regards the belief as mistaken, it is laid upon the historian to explain what happened subsequently by some other cause. Various such attempts have been made and strangely unconvincing most of them are. There cannot be a demonstrative 'proof'. But probability is the guide of life, in religious as well as in ethical decisions. And 'far the least improbable explanation is that what the Christians believed is true and that it did really happen'.[1]

The real evidence for the Resurrection is what has happened in human lives because of it. 'The Church cannot doubt the Resurrection because it cannot doubt its own existence.' What called the Church into being and keeps it in being is the power and presence of the living Christ in the Community of the Holy Spirit. The emergence of the Christian society in its depth and quality of living and its ongoing extension throughout the world, with its saints and martyrs, prophets and evangelists, and the millions of 'ordinary' men and women – a multitude whom no man can number – who have hoped on in the face of despair, who have struggled on and won in the face of difficulty, who have loved on in the face of hatred, who have been sanctified out of self-will, who have shown forth the authentic fruit of the Spirit, and at the last have not been afraid to die – these are the evidence of the Resurrection.

The Apostles believed, and all Christians have believed, that these things were due to the fact that the Lord had risen and was present in the community of his own, because God had raised him from the dead. Either that belief is true – and the whole structure of Christian faith depends on it; without it there could

[1] Alan Richardson, *History Sacred and Profane* (S.C.M. Press), pp. 195ff. This provides an important discussion of the real nature of historical evidence.

K

be no Christianity – or Christianity rests on an illusion. Can a corrupt tree bring forth good fruit?

No orthodox believer could put the case more starkly and cogently than Lord Eccles. 'Either Easter Sunday was a revelation from outside the process of evolution, or Christ's flag should be hauled down and the not disreputable flag of humanism unfurled in its place.'[1]

What is at stake in the Christian affirmation is not only, and indeed not primarily, belief in a future life for ourselves. That belief is derivative from another. Fundamentally, what is at stake is nothing less than the possibility of belief in God. Jesus went to the Cross trusting God to bring him out victorious on the other side and to vindicate the Son of Man. In the final test was that faith discredited? For if Jesus stayed dead, then his God is dead. There is no such God as he believed in, nothing to trust, to hope for or to live for. We are swallowed up in the pit of meaninglessness.

But Easter is the vindication of God. The power that runs the universe is committed to Jesus, and therefore to the cause of man; and its ultimate energies are on his side. Here is a disclosure out of the heart of things, from 'outside the process of evolution'. Here is the guarantee that the world is more than a closed system of physical determinants – though these, Christians hold, are on their own level a reflection of the faithfulness of God – that it is an open world, alive, purposive, organic to Spirit, with personal Being its constitutive reality – a world in which personal life can grow.

Here is the 'intervention', if we must use that word, of the living God of the Bible and of Christ himself in the processes of space/time in a uniquely self-revealing act– in the true sense a 'miraculous' event. Christians are perfectly free to suspend judgement about some of the 'miracles' recorded in the Gospels or elsewhere in the Bible;[2] but on *this* miracle Christian faith is

[1] op. cit. p. 94.
[2] In these we may include the miraculous embellishments of the Resurrection story itself in Matthew – the earthquake, the descending angels, the 'walking' of the dead.

founded. *In that sense* there is not and never can be any purely naturalistic or 'non-miraculous' Christianity.

*   *   *

But the Resurrection faith has its corollaries. All the teaching of Jesus about true life – eternal life – in its true relationship with the living God, no less than his understanding of his own destiny, points forward beyond the limits of our mortality. God is not the God of the dead but of the living. It points forward to a fulfilment beyond death, in fellowship with God and other spirits – the Communion of Saints, the forgiveness of sins and the resurrection unto eternal life. But this is not simply a fact about *homo sapiens*. Death is the 'natural' end of human life. The life beyond of Christian expectation is a 'supernatural' gift of grace, the gift of God through the risen Christ. The expectation rests on faith in the God who raised Jesus Christ from the dead.

20

AND SITTETH AT THE RIGHT HAND OF THE FATHER

I ascend unto my Father and your Father – John **20**. 17;
Luke **24**. 51

WHEN the creed says, 'he ascended into heaven and sit-
teth at the right hand of God the Father', that is obvi-
ously symbolic language. As a literal statement of fact
it would be nonsense. Heaven is not a place above the clouds,
it is a spiritual condition; and God is not seated on a throne 'up
there'. When we are dealing with spiritual realities and the ultimate mysteries of God's being and action, we can speak only
in imagery and symbol – as the Bible, in fact, does from cover
to cover.

Much modern misunderstanding of the Bible, and of some
of the phrases in the creeds of Christendom, is due to treating
as actual description what is poetry, symbolism or 'myth' – to
go no further, 'he came down from heaven'. There is no other
language that we can use, but we must recognize it for what it
is. 'There's a friend for little children above the bright blue sky.'
As a literal statement that is just not true: but can there be any
better way of conveying the truth which it is trying to express?

Not all truth is scientific truth. The human mind is conditioned
by space and time and it cannot, perhaps, therefore think in
other terms. It is bound to use spatial and temporal metaphors
– to speak of 'here' and 'there', or 'before' and 'after' – when it
tries to think about spiritual realities which are not spatio-
temporal at all.

The story of Christ's Ascension into heaven and exaltation at
the right hand of God is thus an imaginative presentation of
Christian faith in the Lordship of Christ as God's final word in
man's life and destiny. What it *means* is that 'God highly

exalted him and gave unto him the name which is above every name, that in the Name of Jesus every knee should bow . . . and every tongue should confess that Jesus Christ is Lord, to the glory of God the Father' (Philippians 2. 9–11, *R.V.*). It conveys the ultimate insight of Christian faith in the form of a story – that is, of a 'myth'.

The man in the pew is often perplexed and worried by the way in which current theological writing uses words like 'myth' and 'mythological'. He thinks they mean 'mythical' or just 'imaginary'. When he hears a phrase like 'the Christian myth', what it suggests to him is the Christian fairy-story, with the implication that it is not 'true', that the Christian events did not really happen, that it was all invented by human credulity in a pre-critical, pre-scientific age. But of course that is not what the theologians mean.

Mythological does not mean legendary. When we say 'Crucified under Pontius Pilate', that is a statement of historical fact, for which we can adduce historical evidence. Round it there may gather legendary material – there may be traces of that in Matthew's narrative – purporting to add further historical facts. Such legends can, at any rate in principle, be checked, as being true history or not, as having really happened or not, by the tools of historical evidence and criticism. But when we say he was crucified 'for us', or that God commended his love to us in that while we were yet sinners Christ died for us, we have passed beyond historical facts to meanings, to what Christian faith finds in these events – and this is not a matter of 'true' or 'legendary', in the sense in which we can say about his death that it either really happened or didn't happen. But that is not to say that it is 'untrue'. It conveys truth, but a different kind of truth, which cannot be 'proved' or disproved by the historian.

In its Christian usage (and in its use by Plato) a myth can best be described as a story conveying ultimate spiritual meanings – the 'mysteries of God's being and action' – which transcends scientific or purely logical thought and the deepest intuitions of Christian faith; and here, as an American scholar puts it, 'myth is the only alternative to silence'. There is no other way of conveying that intuition. Thus what might be called 'the Christian myth' itself – 'the Son of God for us men and for our salvation came down from heaven and suffered and rose again and is now exalted at the right hand of God' – is 'the irreplaceable symbol of what God did in Jesus and the event which happened round him'; and on this depends our existence as Christians. 'To deny the exaltation of Christ at God's right hand is to deny not only an essential element in the Christian faith, but also the existential reality of the Christian life'.

We are right to try, with the tools of historical criticism, to strip off false or legendary elements from the events recorded in the Gospels. But the Gospel itself cannot be 'demythologized'. The demand for a 'modern', up-to-date creed, expressed in the language of rational common sense or the categories of natural science, is one which Christianity cannot meet. 'Modernized creeds, in terms of common sense or of scientific or philosophical thought' – in other words, 'demythologized' creeds – 'would be vapid, futile and in the profoundest sense untrue'.[1] They would not communicate Christian faith and experience or the truth of Christ as Christians know him.

[1] John Knox, *Myth and Truth* (Carey Kingsgate Press 1967) pp. 63, 72, 81. I append here another recent statement: 'If intellectuals in the twentieth century want a concept of the significance of Jesus Christ that can easily be accepted as scientific or readily identified as historical fact or even understood as demanding a purely intellectual assent (i.e. without the personal commitment of faith), it is the duty of the Church to disappoint them' – Hanson, op. cit., p, 47.

21

AND HE SHALL COME AGAIN IN GLORY

THERE is no point at which traditional orthodoxy is more confused than the 'Second Coming'. Popular religion has inherited ideas, images and symbols drawn from all manner of sources, some biblical and some extraneous; and, in spite of the warning of Jesus himself (Mark **13.** 32; Luke **17.** 23, 24) has often indulged in fantastic calculations about the day and the hour, the 'here' and the 'there'. As so often, imagery and symbol have been treated as though they were descriptive language and then used literally as predictions of actual events in heaven and earth which are due to happen in some far-distant future.

The resulting picture has no *Christian* importance. It has little to do with the religious values revealed in Christ or with his faith in God; it is a pseudo-scientific cosmogony concerned with the 'end of the world' – the material universe – or, in pulpit language, the 'winding up of time'. The whole idea of the time-process having an end – or a beginning either – is almost impossible to grasp. But in fact half the confusion has arisen from using temporal language – before and after, soon or late – about trans-historical, spiritual realities which, as Jesus said, are not 'here' or 'there', not events in the causal sequence of history.[1]

---

[1] 'The future tenses are only an accommodation of language. There is no Coming of the Son of Man "after" the coming in Galilee and Jerusalem, for there is no before or after in the eternal order. The Kingdom of God in its full reality is not something which will happen after other things have happened. It is that to which men awake when the order of space and time no longer limits their vision. The "Day of the Son of Man" stands for the timeless fact . . . That which cannot be experienced within history is symbolized by the picture of a coming event, and its timeless quality is expressed as pure simultaneity in time – "as the lightning flashes".' (C. H. Dodd, *History and the Gospel*, p. 108.)

Yet Christian expectation of the Parousia runs through every stratum of the tradition. It shines from every book in the New Testament, where, however, it has a profoundly religious content. It is not mere cosmological speculation; and it is a recurrent theme in the Lord's own teaching, from which it cannot possibly be excised. It can hardly be doubted that it derives, in some form or another, from his own mind. Is it possible to recover from the Gospels what Jesus himself believed and taught about it?

The Gospels know nothing about a 'second' Coming. Like all the other books in the New Testament, what they speak about is the Coming, or, alternatively, the Day of the Son of Man, or the Son of Man in his Day. The first believers expected an immediate *Parousia* whereby Christ would come into his own and would be manifested in glory to establish the new age of God. (They were not thinking about 'the end of the world'. The point is that this was to be the Coming of *Christ*, with all that it meant for those who believed in him, not a kind of theological thriller but a joyful Christian hope and expectation. Though they used symbols of physical catastrophe – lightning and clouds, falling stars and so forth – taken over from popular apocalypses, their real concern was religious – the fulfilment of his redemptive work in the lives of men.) Our Lord had almost certainly used language about his own appearance in glory and the vindication of the Son of Man – the Coming of the Son of Man in power. But had he in fact envisaged *two* Comings, the Resurrection and another still to be?

How the eschatology of the primitive Church came to be formed can be traced, as Dodd shows, from the sermons of Peter reported in *Acts*. Jesus had said before the High Priest 'Ye shall see the Son of Man sitting at the right hand of the Power (i.e. God) and coming with the clouds of heaven' (Mark **14**. 62)

Now Peter affirmed that *by the Resurrection* God had made Jesus both Lord and Christ, and that he was exalted at God's right hand (Acts **2**. 33, 36). The interval of the conventional 'forty days' between the Resurrection and the Ascension belongs to a later stage in the tradition. In St. John the Resurrection and Ascension are regarded as two moments in the same fact (John 20. 17), and so, it seems, by Luke when he wrote his Gospel. By the time that *Acts* came to be written they had been separated by forty days, just as the coming of the Spirit was postponed, as it were, till Pentecost.[1] The primitive belief was, apparently, that the first half of what Jesus had predicted was already fulfilled by the Resurrection; he was risen, ascended into heaven and seated at the right hand of God. But he had yet to appear on the clouds of heaven – and this they expected to happen at any moment. There are grounds enough in the Gospels for belief in an *imminent* coming of the Christ, but none for a Coming in some far-distant future, as the end-term of historical evolution – 'the one far-off divine event'.

The Parousia did not come in the way they looked for, and the vivid expectation of the first days gradually receded into the background. In the Fourth Gospel and in *Ephesians* the Parousia is envisaged in changed terms as the Presence of Christ through the Spirit in the Church. Had he, then, 'come' already, in the *Koinonia*?[2]

Jesus certainly seems to have spoken about the Day of the Son of Man in the future just as he had spoken about the coming or fulfilment of the Kingdom in the future. And either he or his hearers and reporters had used the current apocalyptic imagery – though he himself was a prophet, not an apocalyptist. Mark 13 (and its parallels in Matthew and Luke) is now regarded by practically all scholars as an early Christian

[1] For a recent study of the two streams of tradition about Pentecost, see N. Micklem, *My Cherry Tree* (Geoffrey Bles, 1966), pp. 161–79.

[2] A late and pseudonymous writer (2 Peter 3. 8ff.) tried to use mathematical ingenuity to allay the disappointment of hope deferred. God never intended the Coming to be immediate, because with God one day equals a thousand years; so it may be a very long time yet! But this is a perfectly hopeless way of dealing with spiritual, timeless realities.

Apocalypse, existing independently in written form, reflecting subsequent Christian experience (persecution, the siege of Jerusalem and so on) into which the evangelists have inserted some authentic sayings of Jesus. This, of course, means that it must not be taken as a detailed prediction in the Lord's own words of what is going to happen before 'the end comes'.

There is much to suggest that he did think and speak about an immediate winding up of the present order; and the 'thorough-going eschatologists' have made all that can be made of this material (drawn almost entirely from M) and, indeed, more than can rightly be made of it, to the virtual exclusion of everything else. But if this was his *whole* thought, then there could have been no ethical teaching, only a provisional 'ethic of the interim'. And in that case, the Sermon on the Mount and all the 'ethical' teaching ascribed to him in the Gospels and elsewhere in the New Testament must have been thought up by the Church later and then read back into the mouth of Jesus. Indeed 'a heroic piece of destructive criticism'! Side by side there is much in the ethical teaching (and in the presuppositions of the parables), which assumes that civilization will go on.

There are in fact 'two diverse strains in the teaching of Jesus – one which appears to contemplate an indefinite continuance of human life under historical conditions; the other, its speedy end. We do not possess the key to their reconciliation' (Dodd). This dialectic of seeming contradictories reflects the creativity of his mind. It may, perhaps, be regarded as inherent in the total fact which we call the Incarnation.

Jesus believed that in himself and the Kingdom whose arrival he proclaimed there was, as it were, a meeting of two worlds, an intersection of two planes of reality. (That seems to be what is meant when theologians speak of 'an eschatological situation'.) The world was confronted by its supreme crisis. According as it responded or refused, so would God be revealed in salvation or in judgement. *These* events, his own life and death, would be working out their consequences in all history.[1] But there is no evidence that he thought of these as superimposed by some 'second' divine act or except as arising out of his own ministry; the judgement on Jerusalem, for example, or his own vindication in glory. 'There is in his teaching no Coming of the Son of Man which does not refer to *this* ministry, its climax and its consequences.'[2]

Jesus went to his death certain that he would be vindicated. But, as Dr. Robinson has maintained, 'for Jesus, as originally for Mark, the Rising of the Son of Man out of suffering and death and the Coming of the Son of Man on the clouds of heaven are alternative expressions of the same thing. They are certainly so interpreted by John'.[3]

If that is indeed so, then popular orthodoxy and the language of some of the familiar hymns on the whole matter seems to have gone astray, and some radical re-thinking is now required.

There is, however, an entirely real sense in which Christians may 'look for the Coming of the Lord'. The emphasis ought to rest, not on the notion of an absentee Christ, one day to come back again, but on that of a living Christ who is always present, who ever comes in judgement and deliverance in every critical 'moment to decide' in private life and in the life of nations, the Christ that is and the Christ that is to be, whose full meaning has yet to be discovered, who, as St. Paul said, is coming to his fulfilment, in whom humanity has yet to grow up to the measure

[1] 'Christians (and perhaps Jesus himself) – were using current imagery and forms of thinking – after all, no others were open to them. What they *meant* by them was at least this – the way to eternal life depends on your attitude to Jesus (you are "judged" by that). We cannot think about an imminent "end of the world", which in any case is a spatio-temporal metaphor for spiritual realities. The parousia meant for them the new age – the God-planned way of living. Our need is to find the real way of living – "eternal life" – and it is our attitude to and obedience to Jesus or otherwise which decides whether we find it and enter it or not.' (From Fenton's *St. Matthew* – Penguin, p. 22.)

[2] J. A. T. Robinson (Bishop of Woolwich), *Jesus and his Coming* (S.C.M., 1957), p. 81. This book offers a valuable detailed study of the evidence in our sources.

[3] Op. cit. p. 167, note 2.

of the stature of his completion. (Ephesians **4.** 13). He has come, he is always coming, and is yet to come.[1]

But here, too, as in the Resurrection, what is fundamental is faith in God. Is the God in whom he believed the real God, maker of heaven and earth and of all things visible and invisible? Is the world itself the kind of world, ultimately ruled and sustained by the Goodness and Love manifest in Jesus, in which he can come into his own? For that is what it means to believe in God, the Father of our Lord Jesus Christ, WHOSE KINGDOM SHALL HAVE NO END.

* * *

Mark's narrative of the Resurrection breaks off in the middle of a sentence (Mark **16.** 8); either the last page was lost at an early stage in the manuscript transmission, or *possibly* for theological reasons. (For discussion of this, see any recent commentary.) That gives an abrupt ending to the story. But in fact the story was only just beginning.

[1] The fundamental importance for Christian faith and experience of the N.T. language about the Coming and the End is its witness to the 'finality' and all-sufficiency of Christ himself. 'Now that Jesus has risen the New Order is here; the Church stands between the Cross and the End. His coming is so important that the only really important thing that can happen after it is the end of the world. If we ask the N.T. what sort of significance Jesus has, it does not reply, in a philosophical, Aristotelian way, that he is the second *hypostasis* in a *trias*, of one substance with the Father as touching his Godhead. But it does say, in its Jewish eschatological way, that his significance is unlimited. He is literally of the last importance, for he is God's last Word and last Act. In its own way the N.T. appears to be saying much the same thing as the Nicene Creed says in its very different way' – Hanson, op. cit. pp. 44, 45.

EPILOGUE

THE New Testament, as we have seen, is the creation of the believing community, which, in its turn, is created and renewed by it. Written out of faith, it requires faith – not the mere acceptance of propositions or the willingness to repeat the 'correct' phrases, but that moral decision, that personal commitment, by which Jesus is recognized as Lord. But that faith is mediated and sustained by membership in the community of believers. 'There is no such thing as a solitary Christian' (John Wesley). If he wants to know who Jesus Christ is, a man must go where the believers are; he can never learn as a detached spectator. He can only possess himself of the truth of Christ within the community of the Holy Spirit. The faith of the New Testament is a shared faith. Christian faith and experience are communal, and bound up with membership in the Church.

I do not, of course, mean that a man must submit himself to the psychological workings of mass-suggestion, sinking himself in a kind of religious collective till he comes to make its slogans his own, abjuring his personal responsibility and repeating at second hand the beliefs of others. (It must be true because 'everybody' says so!) What I mean is something far deeper, which involves the whole nature of human personality and of Christianity, which is essentially the religion of personality. As the self needs other selves in order to realize its selfhood, so the Christian needs other Christians in order to apprehend Christianity. That indeed was how Christian faith was born. It was not that the disciples of Jesus decided to form a voluntary society in order to propagate a belief of which they were independently convinced. The society and the belief were born together in the constitutive experience of Pentecost. It was through knowing his Spirit in their midst, uniting them with him and with one another in a new relationship to God that they recognized Jesus as Lord and Christ. They did not so know him apart from the Church. Had it not been for that corporate experience, the Gospel story would never have been written.

Whether Jesus intended to 'found a Church', as an ecclesiastical institution, is a question which has to be answered with due reserve. There is simply not the evidence for an unequivocal answer, for we may not know what his innermost thoughts were. But the weight of probability is against it. Few scholars, at any rate, would now feel able to claim with the confidence of earlier students that he laid down regulations in advance, or prescribed the forms of a church-organization, or even that he foresaw the Church in its subsequent historical development. ('Tell it to the church [or 'congregation' – *N.E.B.*]' in Matthew **18.** 17 is everywhere now regarded as secondary, the reflection of later Christian discipline. The command to go and baptize all nations in Matthew **28.** 19, 20 is attributed to the Christ after the Resurrection, not to Jesus during his earthly life.)

But in a real sense the Church was there when he gathered disciples around him in an intimate relationship to himself as the nucleus of the restored and redeemed 'remnant', the core, as it were, of the true people of God; and in the last night before he suffered, as he bound them into a covenant relationship with himself and with one another by the sacrificial rite of the Loaf and the Cup. The Crucifixion shattered that community. But when he was restored to them in forgiveness (cf. John **21**) the community was revived and reconsolidated in far closer intimacy than before. The two events are indeed inseparable. The birth of the Christian Church and the Resurrection are two aspects of the same fact: the risen Christ is Christ in his Church.

'Christ loved the church and gave himself for it' (Ephesians **5.** 25) in the sense, at least, that he called it into being by his life of love, his suffering and his triumph. So intimate is the relationship that St. Paul speaks of the Church as Christ's Body, the instrument of his self-expression. Without the Church he is not the Christ. As St. Augustine was to say later, the whole Christ (*totus Christus*) is Christ in his Body. The existential fact of the Christian community is the source of its fundamental theology. It was not merely that 'someone' had risen again. The point is, this was the resurrection *of Jesus*; and now the disciples understood who he was – that in him God was at work in the life of man and that he was the God-sent Fountain of the new life, the Word made flesh, the 'only-begotten' Son. 'In him was life and the life was the light of men' (John **1.** 4).

Modern secular man must face the questions 'Why is the Christian Church here at all, and what is the reality to which it points?' The Church as it exists in history is the visible 'presence' of Christ in a world in which he is not yet fully acknowledged. In its attempts to incorporate itself, in successive stages and forms in the course of history, it has been exposed to abuses and corruptions and the 'contagion of the world's slow stain'; and the holy Church is composed of sinful men. Yet within and beneath whatever is base and perishable is the inexhaustible, irreducible Person, the Source and Centre of Christian faith and experience. We cannot predict what shapes, what embodiments the Church may be led to assume in the future years. Christianity is still in its infancy. But yesterday, today and forever its life is in One who, as St. Paul said, is in all ways coming to his fulfilment (Ephesians **1.** 23) the Christ who is and the Christ who is to be.